ROYAL BIRKDALE

THE 146TH OPEN
Card of the Championship Course

Hole	Par	Yards	Hole	Par	Yards
1	4	448	10	4	402
2	4	422	11	4	436
3	4	451	12	3	183
4	3	199	13	4	499
5	4	346	14	3	200
6	4	499	15	5	542
7	3	177	16	4	438
8	4	458	17	5	567
9	4	416	18	4	473
Out	34	3,416	In	36	3,740
			Total	70	7,156

D1061437

THE OPEN

146TH ROYAL BIRKDALE

Aurum Press
74-77 White Lion Street, London N1 9PF

Published 2017 by Aurum Press

Copyright 2017 R&A Championships Limited

Course illustration by Strokesaver

Project coordinator: Sarah Wooldridge
Additional thanks to:
NTT Data
Colin Callander
Peter Kollmann

A CIP catalogue record for this book is available
from the British Library

ISBN-13: 978 1 78131 730 3

Designed and produced by Davis Design
Colour retouching by Luciano Retouching Services, Inc.
Printed in Slovenia by Svet Print d.o.o.

THE OPEN
146TH ROYAL BIRKDALE

EDITOR
Andy Farrell

WRITERS AND PHOTOGRAPHERS

Writers	Getty Images	The R&A	Golf Editors
Peter Dixon	Andrew Redington	Ross Kinnaird	Maxx Wolfson
Andy Farrell	Stuart Franklin	David Cannon	Matt Eades
John Hopkins	Christian Petersen	Warren Little	Mark Trowbridge
Lewine Mair	Gregory Shamus	Richard Heathcote	Richard Martin-Roberts
Art Spander	Dan Mullan	Matt Lewis	Brendan Kemp
Alistair Tait		Tom Dulat	Rob Harborne
		Stan Badz	
		Chris Condon	

Foreword

By Jordan Spieth

What an incredible honour it is to be the Champion Golfer of the Year.

Being presented with the Claret Jug will be one of the most memorable moments of my career. We look forward to this exceptional event every year, with The Open's deep history and prized trophy. Part of what makes this win so special is the enthusiasm of the spectators this year at Royal Birkdale, who came out in record numbers. They were some of the most respectful and knowledgeable fans in the world, and as players we very much appreciate their support.

I want to thank the membership at Royal Birkdale for allowing us to tear up their course for a few days. What an incredible venue. And sincere thanks to The R&A for always putting on a world-class Championship.

It was an unforgettable final round. I genuinely enjoyed the battle with Matt Kuchar. He is a class act and I will never forget his encouraging smile when I finally made it to the 13th green — something that speaks to the kind of man he is. He was a formidable competitor and I look forward to many more rounds with him.

I would like to specifically thank my caddie, Michael Greller, for keeping me in the race after a not quite ideal start to Sunday. He deserves a lot of credit for keeping my head straight. Along with Michael, the support of my family and my team has been instrumental in allowing me to pursue this career and helped lead me to this moment.

Winning The Open was truly a dream come true. I will enjoy taking great care of the Claret Jug this year in America, and I will continue working hard to try and win it again in the years ahead. I am honoured to be in this company.

The Championship Committee

CHAIRMAN
Clive T Brown

DEPUTY CHAIRMAN
Peter Cowell

COMMITTEE

Peter Arthur	Neil McConachie
Andrew Bathurst	Peter McEvoy OBE
Nick Ellis	Paul McKellar
Brian Fleming	David Meacher
John Louden	Anne O'Sullivan
Charlie Maran	Rona Walker

CHIEF EXECUTIVE
Martin Slumbers

EXECUTIVE DIRECTOR – CHAMPIONSHIPS
Johnnie Cole-Hamilton

EXECUTIVE DIRECTOR – GOVERNANCE
David Rickman

Introduction

By Clive T Brown,
Chairman of the Championship Committee of The R&A

The 146th Open at Royal Birkdale will be remembered for a remarkable performance by Jordan Spieth, who was crowned Champion Golfer of the Year for the first time following a three-shot victory over his fellow American Matt Kuchar.

On his way to lifting the iconic Claret Jug, Spieth became the first player to post scores under 70 in every round of an Open staged at Royal Birkdale and only the 12th to hold at least a share of the lead after each round of the Championship.

I would also like to congratulate Alfie Plant, the young England international, who won the Silver Medal as the leading amateur.

A record-breaking crowd of 235,000, including 30,000 fans under the age of 25, were enthralled by events at Royal Birkdale, setting an attendance record for a Championship staged outside of St Andrews and making it the largest ever held in England. I would like to thank everyone who came along to Royal Birkdale for making it a very special Championship.

The Open is highly regarded as a world-class sporting event and there are so many people who deserve a great deal of praise and acknowledgement for delivering the Championship to such a high standard. I wish to thank the members and staff of Royal Birkdale Golf Club and the thousands of volunteers who worked tirelessly before and during the Championship to ensure its smooth running.

We now look forward to The 147th Open at Carnoustie, another one of the world's finest links courses. It will be a pleasure to welcome fans there for the first time since it last hosted the Championship in 2007, when Padraig Harrington achieved a memorable victory.

Bryson DeChambeau

Sung-Hoon Kang

Callum Shinkwin

Jbe' Kruger

146TH
ROYAL BIRKDALE

AMERICA

Quicken Loans National	29 June-2 July
Kyle Stanley, USA	
Charles Howell III, USA	
Martin Laird, Scotland	
Sung-Hoon Kang, Korea	
The Greenbrier Classic	6-9 July
Xander Schauffele, USA	
Robert Streb, USA	
Jamie Lovemark, USA	
Sebastian Muñoz, Colombia	
John Deere Classic	13-16 July
Bryson DeChambeau, USA	

THE
OPEN®
QUALIFYING SERIES

SOUTH AFRICA

Joburg Open	23-26 Feb
Darren Fichardt, South Africa	
Stuart Manley, Wales	
Paul Waring, England	

Austin Connelly

Ian Poulter

Stuart Manley

Richie Ramsay

EUROPE

HNA Open de France	29 June-2 July

Peter Uihlein, USA
Alexander Björk, Sweden
Mike Lorenzo-Vera, France

Dubai Duty Free Irish Open	6-9 July

Richie Ramsay, Scotland
Ryan Fox, New Zealand
David Drysdale, Scotland

Aberdeen Asset Management Scottish Open	13-16 July

Callum Shinkwin, England
Matthieu Pavon, France
Andrew Dodt, Australia

FINAL QUALIFYING

Gailes Links	4 July

Connor Syme[a], Scotland
Julian Suri, USA
Ryan McCarthy[P], Australia

Hillside	4 July

Haydn McCullen, England
Nicholas McCarthy, England
Adam Hodkinson, England

Notts (Hollinwell)	4 July

Joe Dean, England
Mark Foster, England
Laurie Canter, England

Royal Cinque Ports	4 July

Matthew Southgate, England
Robert Dinwiddie, England
Austin Connelly[P], Canada

Woburn	4 July

Shiv Kapur, India
Toby Tree, England
Ian Poulter, England

[a]Denotes amateur   [P]Qualified after play-off

JAPAN

Mizuno Open	25-28 May

Chan Kim, USA
Michael Hendry, New Zealand
Adam Bland, Australia
KT Kim, Korea

SINGAPORE

SMBC Singapore Open	19-22 Jan

Prayad Marksaeng, Thailand
Younghan Song, Korea
Phachara Khongwatmai, Thailand
Jbe' Kruger, South Africa

AUSTRALIA

Australian Open	17-20 Nov 2016

Ashley Hall, Australia
Cameron Smith, Australia
Aaron Baddeley, Australia

EXEMPT COMPETITORS

Sergio Garcia

Justin Rose

Rory McIlroy

Rickie Fowler

Name, Country	Category
Byeong Hun An, Korea	6
Daniel Berger, USA	4,12
Richard Bland, England	5
Paul Broadhurst, England	24
Wesley Bryan, USA	4
Kent Bulle, USA	15
Rafa Cabrera Bello, Spain	4,5,17
Paul Casey, England	4,12
Roberto Castro, USA	12
Yikeun Chang, Korea	16
Kevin Chappell, USA	4,12
Luca Cianchetti[a], Italy	27
Stewart Cink, USA	1,2
Darren Clarke, Northern Ireland	1,2
John Daly, USA	1
Jason Day, Australia	4,10,11,12
Jason Dufner, USA	10,12
David Duval, USA	1
Harry Ellis[a], England	25
Ernie Els, South Africa	1,2
Tony Finau*, USA	4
Ross Fisher, England	4,5
Matthew Fitzpatrick, England	4,5,17
Tommy Fleetwood, England	4
Rickie Fowler, USA	4,11,17
Dylan Frittelli, South Africa	7
Sergio Garcia, Spain	3,4,5,9,17
Branden Grace, South Africa	4,5
Matthew Griffin, Australia	19
Emiliano Grillo, Argentina	4,12
Bill Haas, USA	3,4
Adam Hadwin, Canada	4
James Hahn*, USA	4
Todd Hamilton, USA	1
Brian Harman, USA	13
Padraig Harrington, Rep of Ireland	1,2
Tyrrell Hatton, England	3,4,5
Scott Hend, Australia	5,18
Russell Henley, USA	13
Charley Hoffman, USA	13
JB Holmes, USA	3,4,12,17
Billy Horschel, USA	4
David Horsey, England	5
Yuta Ikeda, Japan	22
Thongchai Jaidee, Thailand	5
Dustin Johnson, USA	3,4,8,12,17
Zach Johnson, USA	1,2,17
Andrew Johnston, England	3,5
Martin Kaymer, Germany	5,8,17
Giwhan Kim, Korea	16
Si Woo Kim, Korea	4,11,12
Kevin Kisner, USA	4,12
Søren Kjeldsen, Denmark	3,5
Russell Knox, Scotland	4,12
Brooks Koepka, USA	4,8,17
Matt Kuchar, USA	4,12,17

Name, Country	Category
Anirban Lahiri*, India	4
Pablo Larrazábal, Spain	
Paul Lawrie, Scotland	
Tom Lehman, USA	
Marc Leishman, Australia	4
Alexander Levy, France	
Haotong Li, China	5
David Lipsky, USA	
Shane Lowry, Rep of Ireland	
Joost Luiten, Netherlands	5
Sandy Lyle, Scotland	
Hideki Matsuyama, Japan	4,12,2
William McGirt, USA	4,12
Rory McIlroy, Northern Ireland	1,2,3,4,5,10,12,1
Maverick McNealy[a], USA	28
Phil Mickelson, USA	1,2,3,4,12,17
Yusaku Miyazato, Japan	23
Francesco Molinari, Italy	45
Ryan Moore, USA	4,12,17
Kevin Na, USA	1
Alex Noren, Sweden	4,5,6
Shaun Norris, South Africa	23
Sean O'Hair, USA	12
Mark O'Meara, USA	
Thorbjørn Olesen, Denmark	5
Louis Oosthuizen, South Africa	1,2,4,5
Pat Perez, USA	
Thomas Pieters, Belgium	4,5,17
Alfie Plant[a], England	27
Jon Rahm, Spain	4
Patrick Reed, USA	4,12,17
Justin Rose, England	4,8,14,17
Charl Schwartzel, South Africa	4,5,12
Adam Scott, Australia	4,9,12
Webb Simpson, USA	4
Jordan Spieth, USA	4,8,9,12,17
Brendan Steele, USA	13
Henrik Stenson, Sweden	1,2,3,4,5,17
Brandon Stone, South Africa	20
Steve Stricker, USA	3
Andy Sullivan, England	5,17
Hideto Tanihara, Japan	4,22
Justin Thomas, USA	4,12
Jhonattan Vegas, Venezuela	12
Jimmy Walker, USA	4,10,12,17
Jeunghun Wang, Korea	5
Bubba Watson, USA	4,9,12
Lee Westwood, England	5,17
Bernd Wiesberger, Austria	4,5
Danny Willett, England	4,5,9,17
Chris Wood, England	5,6,17
Gary Woodland, USA	4,12
Fabrizio Zanotti, Paraguay	7

2016 Champion Golfer of the Year Henrik Stenson returned the Claret Jug to Martin Slumbers, Chief Executive of The R&A, after being transported to Royal Birkdale in a Mercedes-Benz F 015 Concept Car.

KEY TO EXEMPTIONS FROM THE OPEN QUALIFYING SERIES

Exemptions for 2017 were granted to the following:

(1) The Open Champions aged 60 or under on 23 July 2017.

(2) The Open Champions for 2007-2016.

(3) First 10 and anyone tying for 10th place in The 145th Open Championship at Royal Troon.

(4) The first 50 players on the Official World Golf Ranking for Week 21, 2017, with additional players and reserves drawn from the highest ranked non-exempt players in the weeks prior to The Open.

(5) Final 30 in the Race to Dubai Rankings for 2016.

(6) The BMW PGA Championship winners for 2015-2017.

(7) First 5 European Tour members and any European Tour members tying for 5th place, not otherwise exempt, in the top 20 of the Race to Dubai Rankings on completion of the 2017 BMW International Open.

(8) The US Open Champions for 2013-2017.

(9) The Masters Tournament Champions for 2013-2017.

(10) The PGA Champions for 2012-2016.

(11) THE PLAYERS Champions for 2015-2017.

(12) The top 30 players from the 2016 FedExCup points list.

(13) First 5 PGA TOUR members and any PGA TOUR members tying for 5th place, not exempt in the top 20 of the PGA TOUR FedExCup Points List for 2017 on completion of the 2017 Travelers Championship.

(14) The 2016 Olympic Golf Gold medallist.

(15) The 111th VISA Open de Argentina 2016 Champion.

(16) The 2017 KOLON Korean Open Champion and runner-up.

(17) Playing members of the 2016 Ryder Cup Teams.

(18) First and anyone tying for 1st place on the Order of Merit of the Asian Tour for 2016.

(19) First and anyone tying for 1st place on the Order of Merit of the PGA Tour of Australasia for 2016.

(20) First and anyone tying for 1st place on the Order of Merit of the Southern Africa PGA Sunshine Tour for 2016.

(21) The Japan Open Champion for 2016.

(22) First 2 and anyone tying for 2nd place, on the Official Money List of the Japan Golf Tour for 2016.

(23) First 2 and anyone tying for 2nd place, not exempt having applied OQS Japan, in a cumulative money list taken from all official 2017 Japan Golf Tour events up to and including the 2017 Japan Tour Championship.

(24) The Senior Open Champion for 2016.

(25) The Amateur Champion for 2017.

(26) The US Amateur Champion for 2016.

(27) The European Amateur Champions for 2016 and 2017.

(28) The Mark H McCormack Medal (WORLD AMATEUR

Birkdale a National Treasure

By Andy Farrell

In the light of another exhilarating Open at Royal Birkdale — huge crowds, record-breaking golf and a thrilling finale — it is worth revisiting the words of Henry Longhurst on the famous links.

Five decades or so ago, reading Longhurst in *The Sunday Times* was as much of a ritual for many as church and Sunday lunch, but he also had a long-running column in *Golf Illustrated*. In one piece Longhurst made the case for a national course for England, conceding that St Andrews already held that status for Scotland. He also added that if there was to be a permanent venue for The Open, in the manner of the FA Cup final at Wembley or the tennis at Wimbledon, then it would have to be the Old Course.

But if there was a venue south of the border that could share the burden of regularly hosting the game's greatest Championship, it was Birkdale, Longhurst declared. With plenty of accommo-

The Open at Royal Birkdale — with the 18th hole on right.

dation in Southport, good transport links with Hillside train station nearby, Hillside Golf Club to help with qualifying, and room for spectator amenities, perhaps even a permanent Press room, he thought it had everything — except perhaps for the state-of-the-art gym provided for the players by The R&A this year.

"The more I think of it, the more I should choose Birkdale," he summed up. "It is a course of quality, right in the centre of a populous and golf-conscious area, and, not lightly to be forgotten, it is reasonably difficult to get into Birkdale without paying!"

There is no danger of that these days, but if The 146th Open is any guide, Birkdale is more popular than ever with both the players and fans. With more than 235,000 spectators over the week, this was the third most attended Championship after those at St Andrews in 2000 and 2015.

This particular Longhurst column appeared in the week after The Open in 1961 but must have been written beforehand, otherwise there would surely have been a mention of the late Arnold Palmer's remarkable victory. A year earlier he had narrowly missed out on the Claret Jug on his debut

Thomas Pieters plays from the island of green in the ring bunker at the seventh hole during a practice round.

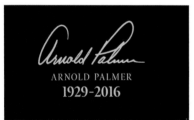

ARNOLD PALMER
1929-2016

ROBERTO DE VICENZO
1923-2017

at St Andrews. Here he was not to be denied, posting a string of birdies to start his second round despite a roaring gale, calling a penalty on himself for a ball that moved in a bunker, unseen by any other soul, and saving a par in the third round by extracting himself from the gorse to two feet.

But his most famous escape came from a bush on the 15th hole (now the 16th) when his Scottish caddie, Tip Anderson, had urged a more conservative recovery. "I remember the look of horror Tip gave me when I declined the wedge and reached for a six-iron, intending to go for the green," Palmer recalled.

"The thing was, I could see the ball very clearly and reasoned that if I could get the club face on the ball cleanly, I could get myself out of trouble. I swung as hard as I could, waited a second, and looked up, watching my ball soar high and settle on the putting surface up the hill, 15 feet shy of the hole. The spectators massed there let out thunderous applause."

With that shot, as much as his one-stroke victory over Dai Rees, Palmer's status as a hero was assured in Britain as well as the United States. "It is doubtful that there was a man present at Birkdale who wanted Palmer to lose," Longhurst reported.

Fellow golf writer Pat Ward-Thomas observed: "The very nature

The tee at the eighth hole is found in one of the wilder spots of the 4,000-year-old Sefton dune system.

of his golf suggested a man fighting to overcome great odds, a man unafraid of challenge. Danger was his inspiration. The fact that he embodied toughness and confidence, and was adventurous besides, made him particularly attractive."

A plaque by the bush has long commemorated the shot and his autograph adorned a number of the grandstands at The 146th Open in memory of "The King" — the same honour given to the late Roberto de Vicenzo, the charming player from Argentina who was the Champion Golfer of the Year for 1967.

Yet without Palmer, who won again at Royal Troon in 1962, would The Open have grown into one of the world's greatest sporting events, as it is today? In his autobiography, *A Golfer's Life*, Palmer reflected: "It has been said that my accomplishments at Birkdale helped spark new American interest in The Open, which admittedly was suffering some from the absence of most of the top American players.

"If that's so, I'm glad I could make a valuable contribution, because The Open really is unlike any golf tournament in the world, and its place in the golf firmament, with its storied history and great traditions, was crucial to the growth and development of the modern game."

That American influence continues with Jordan Spieth joining not just Palmer but Lee Trevino, Johnny Miller, Tom Watson and Mark O'Meara as a Champion Golfer at Birkdale. Note the connection with Augusta National — four of the six are Masters champions and Miller, as a three-time runner-up, perhaps should have been. Surely it is no coincidence that the two courses share the ability to test the finest players of the day, as well as allow those of a lesser pedigree to thoroughly enjoy their round.

Spieth's charge to victory, following a cool-headed use of the Rules to make his own great escape at the 13th, could certainly be described as Palmeresque. At other times he plotted his way

The 12th hole, a gem of a par three, was created by Fred W Hawtree ahead of The Open in 1965.

ROYAL BIRKDALE CHAMPIONS

1954	Peter Thomson
1961	Arnold Palmer
1965	Peter Thomson
1971	Lee Trevino
1976	Johnny Miller
1983	Tom Watson
1991	Ian Baker-Finch
1998	Mark O'Meara
2008	Padraig Harrington
2017	Jordan Spieth

around the links in a manner of Peter Thomson. The Australian won the first and the last of his five Claret Jugs at Birkdale and, rather than flogging himself on the practice range, would often prepare by thinking about his game sitting in an armchair. Spieth did some more modern research while sitting at home by watching much of the early television coverage and formulating a game-plan from there.

Set on a dune system that dates back 4,000 years and that is home to a wide variety of flora and fauna — natterjack toads, skylarks, sand lizards *et al.* — Birkdale's layout has continually evolved over the years. Though the club first moved to the Birkdale Hills in 1897, JH Taylor and Fred G Hawtree laid out the basis of the modern course in the 1930s, when the art deco clubhouse, designed to look like a sailing ship amid the dunes, was built.

After The Open in 1961, Hawtree's son, Fred W, added a gem of a new par three at the 12th to replace the old 17th. At the same time a number of tees were moved, paths laid and dunes moulded to allow for better spectator movement and viewing. It all underlined Longhurst's assertion that Birkdale was a premier venue.

A golden decade followed, with The Open returning in 1965 and 1971 and the Ryder Cup being played there in 1965 and 1969 — the

Tommy the poster boy for Southport

Tommy Fleetwood returned home to Southport in the form of his 26-year-old life after finishing fourth at the US Open and winning the HNA Open de France. He grew up in the town — and now lives only an hour away — and advertising posters for The Open featured the local favourite. "My face is on a lot of lamp posts at the moment," he marvelled.

"It's been lovely coming back. I got recognised in the market the other day but there's nobody fainting in the street as I walk past. It's nice being acknowledged. My old school had a banner with all the kids saying 'good luck' and that was very touching. But the banners will be off in a couple of weeks, so best not to get used to it."

Fleetwood learned his golf on the town's municipal layouts and only rarely got to play at Royal Birkdale, though he also occasionally snuck on with his dad for a few holes. "It's one of the best courses in the world, arguably the best Open venue, and you live five minutes away, you're going to try and get on when you can," he admitted.

"You can't sneak on in the places we did now. Once a year I might play it with my mates. But there are so many great courses here. Southport is up there with St Andrews as a golfing town. It's actually a lovely town, I hope people who stay here this week have a nice time."

The Open Camping Village was popular with young fans...

latter famous for Jack Nicklaus's concession of Tony Jacklin's putt that ensured a tied match. A third generation of the Hawtree family, Martin, added his own touch to the course for The Open in 2008, particularly the 17th green onto which Padraig Harrington hit his wondrous five-wood.

As well as being a course where the best players come to the fore — 18 of the world's top 20 made

...as were the bean bags for viewing the big screen.

Stormy skies magnify the dramatic scene at the 18th hole with The Open's huge grandstands and where behind the

the cut this year — Birkdale is also a place where, felicitously, things tend to happen.

There was Liang Huan Lu's second shot at the last hitting a female spectator on the head as he challenged Trevino in 1971; Seve Ballesteros announcing himself with a glorious chip between the bunkers at the 18th in 1976; Hale Irwin having an air shot on a tap-in putt in 1983 only to lose by one; Richard Boxall breaking his leg while tee-ing-off on the ninth hole in 1991; and Justin Rose, then a 17-year-old amateur, holing a pitch shot at the 18th to thunderous applause in 1998.

"It's a great course," Rose reflected on his return in 2008. "I don't know why it creates so much drama, but it does."

In 2017, there was the additional historic ingre-dient of Branden Grace finally lowering the men's major championship record to 62 in the third round — Haotong Li's 63 came a day too late to equal the old record. It had to fall eventually. Once Grace got his putting boots on, given the immaculate state of the greens and the ideal conditions on Saturday, no curse was going to stop him.

Any suggestion that the 62 is a dent in Birkdale's reputation should be dismissed. A well-designed course, set up reasonably, should yield to great golf under benign conditions. There were 43 sub-par rounds from 77 players on Saturday but at other times Birkdale's defences remained strong with only eight players, out of 156, breaking par on Friday.

green Royal Birkdale's famous art deco clubhouse sails amid the dunes.

A decent summer had left the links firm and the rough patchy enough to give the players some room for manoeuvre if they missed the fairways in the right spots. But a couple of overnight soakings softened the ground during the week. A similar pattern of weather occurred at Royal St George's in 1993, the only Open to see two scores of 63 before last year at Royal Troon.

All in all, Birkdale appears to have reached the status of national treasure. While all the players had similar sentiments, local man Tommy Fleetwood perhaps summed up the mood among the competitors. "I'm not just saying it because I'm from Southport, but The Open should be here more than every nine or ten years," he said. "They are the best crowds and this is one of the best tracks in the world. If I had a say, I'd definitely have it more at Birkdale."

Young Fleetwood and old Longhurst would appear to agree.

It was approaching 6.35am on the first day of The 146th Open. The rain was beating down and a gusting crosswind was blowing from left to right across the fairway. Standing on the tee, driver in hand, was Mark O'Meara (above). The winner at Royal Birkdale in 1998, the 60-year-old American had been given the privilege of hitting the Championship's first shot on what is regarded as the toughest opening hole on The Open rota.

As the wind stiffened and O'Meara prepared to take his stance, it was hard not to think that the golfing gods were having a little fun at a former Champion Golfer of the Year's expense. A few moments later the notion was confirmed as O'Meara blocked the ball to the right and winced as he saw it sailing on the wind directly out of bounds.

Perhaps overcompensating with his second ball, the two-time major champion found the bunker down the left of the fairway, flicked it out from an awkward lie and took four more shots to close out the hole. The quadruple-bogey-eight was a shattering blow to a player almost certainly competing in his last Open. "My day was toast and most people still hadn't had their breakfast," a disconsolate O'Meara said after trudging in with an 11-over-par 81.

"I wouldn't say I was overly nervous, but I was not pleased when I hit that shot. My name is on my golf bag, I've won The Open, I've won the Masters, I'm in the Hall of Fame — and then I hit one straight right out of bounds."

If there was consolation to be had, it was that O'Meara was by no means the only player to suffer at the first, a 448-yard par four that had been the second hardest hole on the course in each of its previous two Opens. Johnny Miller, Champion Golfer at Birkdale in 1976, describes the opening tee shot as "one of the most intimidating in the game." It is necessary to be on the right side of the fairway to get a look at the green, but not so far right as to risk going out of bounds when the wind is blowing from the left.

A sign of the difficulty was the fact that the first four three-balls were a combined 16-over-par on the opening hole and that only 24.4 per cent of the

Bryson DeChambeau was among those to suffer at the first.

field was able to find the fairway. The next toughest fairway to hit was the 10th, where 42.3 per cent achieved the feat.

A player in each of the next two groups behind O'Meara's also went out of bounds. The first of them was Maverick McNealy, a 21-year-old amateur from the United States, who confessed that he had never started a round in such conditions; the second was Jeunghun Wang, of Korea.

The first hole did give up an eagle — when America's Charley Hoffman holed his second shot from out of the rough — but there were only 14 birdies and 93 pars on the first day. Most telling was that there were 48 bogeys or worse, including triple-bogey-sevens for Bryson DeChambeau and KT Kim.

Interestingly, with conditions having slightly improved, the hole was not ranked as the most difficult on the first day. That distinction went to the sixth, which played to an average of 4.500. The first was ranked third hardest, with an average of 4.308, with the par-four 16th proving the second most difficult, with an average of 4.327.

What a difference a day makes. With the wind switching direction on Friday, the first hole went

from third most difficult to third easiest. In the third round it was ranked eighth most difficult, with 35 per cent finding the short stuff. And then came Sunday...

It is true to say that Birkdale has a habit of identifying great Champions. While the course can be relatively benign in good conditions, there are moments when it truly bares its teeth, particularly when it sows the seeds of doubt on the first hole. On the final day, with the winds gusting once more, it did just that.

From the last four pairings to take to the course in the last round, only three players walked off with a par. Jordan Spieth, the third-round leader, had a bogey while Dustin Johnson, the world number one, and Hideki Matsuyama, the world number two, fared even worse.

Johnson took three shots to extricate himself from a greenside bunker and walked off with a double-bogey-six from which he never recovered. Matsuyama drove his ball out of bounds and himself immediately out of contention after a triple-bogey-seven.

With a stroke average of 4.286 in the fourth round, the first hole was ranked the most difficult on the final day. The gods would have had it no other way.

Jeunghun Wang searches in vain for his ball at the first.

FIRST ROUND
20 July 2017

American Trio Lead the Way

By Andy Farrell

American golfers have a fine record at Royal Birkdale. Five of the previous six winners of The Open had played in the lead-in tournament in Scotland the week before. And a different five of the last six Champion Golfers of the Year were aged 39 or over.

Crunch all that into a golfing algorithm and the computer says: Matt Kuchar. Or, at least, it did on the opening day of The 146th Open as the 39-year-old American, who finished in a share of fourth place at the Aberdeen Asset Management Scottish Open the previous Sunday, tied for the lead on 65.

In a neat tip of the cap to the likes of Arnold Palmer, Lee Trevino, Johnny Miller, Tom Watson and Mark O'Meara, there were in fact a trio of Americans sharing the top of the leaderboard. First, Jordan Spieth set the five-under-par target and then Brooks Koepka, in his first round since

Matt Kuchar shared the lead with an opening 65.

winning the US Open at Erin Hills, and Kuchar joined the two-time major winner on that mark.

So far in the festival of links golf that culminated in The Open, two things had become apparent: Rory McIlroy was struggling for form after missing the cut in successive weeks, while Spain was holding sway with new sensation Jon Rahm running away with the Dubai Duty Free Irish Open and then Rafa Cabrera Bello beating Callum Shinkwin in a play-off at the Scottish.

Cabrera Bello was handily placed here with an opening 67, but winning the Scottish Open is not necessarily a prerequisite for success, although Phil Mickelson did the double in 2013. Mickelson may have rued his decision to skip the Scottish this year as he opened with a 73 at Birkdale, only to emphasise the point that a competitive run-out by the seaside can be an enormous help in attuning to the bump-and-run game.

Kuchar certainly appreciated having been exposed to the elements at Dundonald. "I was real happy with my performance last week at the Scottish Open," he said. "We had a couple of awfully challenging days. At the 12th hole on Saturday I had 129 yards to the pin and hit a six-iron. I thought

Mark O'Meara opened proceedings, but sadly his drive went out of bounds.

to myself, 'I'm glad I'm over here doing this, you don't get to do this in the States.' So last week was the perfect tune-up."

The exception to the rule, in 2015, was Zach Johnson, who always plays at the John Deere Classic on the PGA Tour the week before and then gets on the charter flight from the Midwest to the old country. It worked two years ago, but here he started with a 75. In 2015, Spieth won the John Deere for the second time having honoured a commitment to play despite taking aim at a third major victory in a row at St Andrews. As it turned out, Spieth missed out on the play-off won by Johnson by a single stroke.

This time Spieth had not played for three weeks. Following his victory at the Travelers Championship, achieved in thrilling fashion by holing a bunker shot to win at the first extra hole, he headed to Cabo in Mexico with some high school friends, also meeting up there with the likes of Michael Jordan and Michael Phelps. "These are guys I've looked up to my entire life," he said. "It was cool that

Jordan Spieth played a fine recovery at the 16th during his 65.

EXCERPTS FROM THE PRESS

"It was a Royal occasion for one of golf's most famous Royals but to the intense disappointment of Tommy Fleetwood there was no command performance. The Southport golfer attracted the kind of galleries that used to follow Tiger Woods in the hope of seeing the local boy's coronation parade towards a first English winner of The Open for 25 years."

—Richard Williamson,
Liverpool Echo

"Gum-chewing gunslinger Jordan Spieth was the last man to win back-to-back majors two years ago. Fun-loving Brooks Koepka is this week trying to take that tag."

—Craig Swan,
Daily Record

"As improbable as it sounds, Ian Poulter told his audience he hadn't realised he was a 'strutter', a label ascribed to him in Scotland last week by Ryder Cup captain Thomas Bjørn, who thought he saw something of a Poulter revival."

—Kevin Garside,
i newspaper

Paul Casey kept his caddie John McLaren amused during his 66.

they included me and asked about what I'm doing. It kind of gives you a nice boost of confidence, if I needed an even bigger head."

Koepka had enjoyed an even longer breather from the game than Spieth. After winning his first major the previous month, he was always due to have a mid-season break, but it is fair to say the celebrations in Las Vegas had an extra potency. "It was fun, we had a good time," was the extent of his report.

Since returning home, Koepka had headed to the gym but had hardly touched a club until he started practising in earnest at Birkdale the previous Saturday. "It was fun to get back inside the ropes and get those competitive juices flowing," he said. "I was in control of my golf ball pretty much all day, just picked up where I left off."

Given Spieth was 23 and Koepka 27, Kuchar was not buying the theory about old-timers winning The Open — McIlroy in 2014 being the exception to this rule. Kuchar said: "I don't pay attention to that, or know if there is a good reason. Certainly, if I was a betting man, I'm not going to rule out Jordan Spieth on that basis. He's got as good a shot as anybody."

It was Spieth that Kuchar was chasing when he set off in the early afternoon, with conditions easing considerably after a cold, wet start and a breezy morning. It took only five holes for him to

Brooks Koepka hit a powerful approach at the 15th on the way to tying for the lead.

The amphitheatre setting of the 14th green made it one of the most popular viewing spots on the course.

Charl Schwartzel drives at the 17th during his 66.

The nattily attired Justin Thomas in the rough on the 16th.

A 67 for Scottish Open winner Rafa Cabrera Bello.

On his Open debut, Austin Connelly opened with a 67.

draw level as he went out in five-under-par 29, one stroke outside the record nine-hole score for The Open set by Denis Durnian at Birkdale in 1983. "I certainly never expected that," he said, "but you take your opportunities where you get them."

As early as the second hole, with the wind still blowing forcefully, Kuchar was able to rekindle his feelings from Dundonald as he hit a six-iron from only 155 yards. "I felt I knew how to play that shot," he explained. It finished 10 feet from the hole and he made the putt for his first birdie. Another six-iron, this time at the 199-yard fourth hole, finished even closer, giving him a five-footer for the first of three birdies in a row. The gentle fifth required only a wedge approach to 10 feet,

First tee nerves for Manley

Shortly after 6.45 on a cold, wet and windy morning, Stuart Manley, a 38-year-old former footballer, hit his first shot in The Open. "I was very nervous on the tee," the Welshman admitted. "The conditions were pretty bad but luckily I made contact, the ball went forward and stayed in bounds."

Four and a bit hours later Manley holed a bunker shot at the 17th for an eagle and birdied the 18th from long range to take the early clubhouse lead in The 146th Open on 68, with Ian Poulter and Justin Rose leading at two-under-par on the course. "I never dreamed of leading The Open, at least so far. It happened so quick it hasn't sunk in."

Manley came up against Michael Owen and Craig Bellamy in junior football and had trials at Manchester United and other clubs. "Deep down I never believed I was good enough, there was too much pressure," he said. "And I love golf so much."

A vital part of Great Britain and Ireland's Walker Cup victory at Ganton in 2003, Manley qualified by finishing runner-up at the Joburg Open. Since then things had not gone his way. He had missed nine of his last 10 cuts, had got flu the previous Sunday and was woken up by his six-month-old baby at 3am. "I was more or less awake anyway," he admitted. "I tried to go to bed early, but I was just too excited to sleep."

Henrik Stenson found trouble on the sixth for a bogey but opened the defence of his title with a 69.

but at the ferocious sixth he needed to thread a hybrid shot onto the green and then saw it run out to within three feet of the hole. "My goal was just to survive the sixth, not to make birdie," he admitted. His fifth birdie came with a nine-iron to five feet at the ninth before he parred the entire second nine.

"I stayed incredibly aggressive, had a couple of opportunities that I wasn't able to convert, but I'm pleased," Kuchar said. "I watched some of the golf this morning and it looked awfully challenging. Anything under par was going to be a good score. Curiously, as the day went on, it seemed the later your tee-time, the better the draw you got."

Paul Casey and Charl Schwartzel were testament to that as they came in with scores of 66 late in the day, while Cabrera Bello and many of those on 67 played in the afternoon, too. By contrast,

Local hero Tommy Fleetwood in a spot of bother on the 17th.

Matthew Fitzpatrick lines up his putt on the 18th green.

Rory McIlroy already had a second bogey by the third hole and was five-over-par after six before he came roaring back.

Rory gets a dressing down from his caddie

On the eve of The Open, Rory McIlroy suggested the odds given on him winning the Claret Jug for a second time were a little insulting. He was determined to prove the bookmakers wrong.

Yet the 2014 Champion Golfer of the Year looked to have taken himself out of contention with 66 holes still to play. When he is at his best, the mercurial Northern Irishman looks invincible. But when his game is off, an air of despondency sometimes descends.

With four bogeys in the first five holes — and another about to occur at the sixth — it took a bold intervention from McIlroy's long-time caddie, JP Fitzgerald, to stop the rot.

"He said to me, 'You're Rory McIlroy, what

the hell are you doing?' the four-time major champion recounted. "At that point, I just mumbled and replied, 'Yeah, whatever.' But it definitely helped. He reminded me who I was, what I was capable of."

From the seventh, McIlroy did not drop a shot. Out in 39, he came home in 32 to finish just one stroke over par and still in the mix. By the end of the round, his jaunty stride was back in place. The next day, he had a 68 in testing conditions and rose from 58th into a tie for sixth.

"In any other circumstance, it might have been a disappointing day, but because of the way it finished I feel great," he said. "There was a lack of self-belief. Somehow, I was able to find it again halfway through."

Ian Poulter, after qualifying at his home club of Woburn, was for a time the clubhouse leader on 67, having set off early in the day.

This was Kuchar's lowest score at The Open in his third visit to Royal Birkdale. In both 1998, when he was the reigning US Amateur champion, and 2008 he had missed the cut, as he did on six of his first seven appearances in The Open. "I had forgotten just how good a golf course it is," he said. "It seems so playable, so fair, so well designed with the different staggering of bunkers. You feel like quality shots are rewarded, you are not going to get a funny kick.

"I know I've been around for a while but I also feel I'm in the prime of my golfing career," he added. "I feel like I have as good a chance as anybody."

Like Kuchar, Spieth did not drop a shot during his round and looked ominously impressive as he went to the turn in 31. He went out mid-morning when the wind was a foe to be respected. It helped that, for the first time on the morning of a tournament round, his coach Cameron McCormick had got him to hit shots on the practice range with a TrackMan device to get a feel for the conditions. "I was able to know how far the ball would travel and then be able to trust it," Spieth explained.

After a three at the par-four second, Spieth made back-to-back birdies at the eighth and ninth holes before a seven-iron to 15 feet set up a two at the par-three 14th. He made a fine up-and-down from a bunker at the 16th and then two-putted for his fifth birdie of the day at the par-five 17th. "I couldn't have done much better," he said. "I missed two greens, and another just on the fringe, in 15 mile-an-hour winds, lots of crosswinds, so that speaks a lot for the ball-striking today."

Having revealed that his coach had given him a piece of mint gum before the round and that as things were going so well he decided to stick with it the whole way, Spieth was asked how the round compared to others in his career. "It could

Fan favourite Andrew 'Beef' Johnston opened with a 69.

Sweden's Alex Noren was well placed on two-under 68.

Spectators look down from a raised platform on Hideki Matsuyama playing his second shot at the fifth hole.

Charley Hoffman briefly tied for the lead during his 67.

be a lot more significant in three days' time than I would consider it right now," he said.

In four previous Opens, Spieth's lowest score was a 66 at St Andrews, while in three previous Opens Koepka had never done better than a 68. Koepka's results had trended in the right direction from a missed cut in 2013 to 67th in 2014 and a top-10 finish in 2015. He missed The Open in 2016 due to an ankle injury, but returned this year as a major champion following his triumph at Erin Hills.

The Floridian first came to prominence on the European Challenge Tour and retains a love of links golf. "Any time I can come across the Pond and play links, it's special, especially after missing last year," he said. "I love the creativity. I see so many different shots and having to pick one is hard. Avoiding the bunkers is the big thing."

But it worked out fine for Koepka at the 17th. Earlier he had claimed just one birdie going out, at the eighth hole, before going three-two-three from the 11th. His only dropped shot came at the 16th after a poor putt and then he found the front-right greenside bunker at the 17th, a popular spot

Kuchar escapes from a bunker at the 17th for yet another par coming home.

all day with the hole cut towards the front of the green. "It was actually a terrible lie," he said. "My caddie told me to get inside 10 feet, that would be pretty good. Luckily enough it went in." That meant an eagle-three and a share of the lead.

Koepka was one of four players to come home in 32, as did Schwartzel with birdies at the last two holes, Thomas Pieters in a 69 and McIlroy. It was quite a turnaround for the Northern Irishman after he bogeyed five of the first six holes. After a talking to from his caddie, McIlroy slowly got himself together, holed a decent putt at the eighth to avoid a sixth bogey, and after birdieing the last two holes he was far more perky than a 71 would otherwise suggest.

On the same score were Justin Rose, the hero of 1998, European Amateur champion Alfie Plant, plus world number one Dustin Johnson and Rickie Fowler. Local favourite Tommy Fleetwood, cheered

Round of the Day: Matt Kuchar – 65

OFFICIAL SCORECARD
THE 146TH OPEN
ROYAL BIRKDALE

Matt KUCHAR
Game 38
Thursday 20 July at 1.37 pm

FOR R&A USE ONLY 38.1

THIS ROUND 65 — ROUND 1 18 HOLE TOTAL 65

VERIFIED

ROUND 1

Hole	1	2	3	4	5	6	7	8	9	Out	10	11	12	13	14	15	16	17	18	In	Total
Yards	448	422	451	199	346	499	177	458	416	3416	402	436	183	499	200	542	438	567	473	3740	7156
Par	4	4	4	3	4	4	3	4	4	34	4	4	3	4	3	5	4	5	4	36	70
Score	4	3	4	2	3	3	3	4	4	36	4	4	3	4	3	5	4	5	4	36	65

Signature of Marker

Signature of Competitor
Matt Kuchar

Thomas Pieters contemplates a putt at the fifth hole.

Irish Open champion Jon Rahm was on 69.

Amateur Champion Harry Ellis struggled to a 77.

on by the largest gallery of all, disappointed with a 76, but Andrew "Beef" Johnston, who became a folk hero at Royal Troon 12 months earlier, was in touch on 69, the same score as Henrik Stenson on the defence of his title. Rahm was also on one-under-par after escaping a possible two-stroke penalty for moving a creeper near his ball in the rough at the 17th hole. Rahm thought it was dead and, therefore, a loose impediment which could be moved without a problem. Despite this not being the case, it was ruled that there was no penalty as he had not improved the lie of the ball or the area of intended swing.

On his last day as a 39-year-old, Casey led the home challenge, birdieing the 16th and 17th holes to finish just one off the lead. "I've always loved this week because my birthday has been on or around it," he said. "I love going to work on my birthday, I genuinely do. And apparently life begins at 40, so maybe that's a good omen for me this week."

Fit from a cycling holiday in the Italian Dolomites, the Arizona-based golfer added: "I love being back in England and Royal Birkdale may be my favourite links of any on the rotation. There are so many cool things about it, just the whole week so far has been perfect."

One day later Casey, among others, found that was no longer the case.

FIRST ROUND LEADERS

HOLE	1	2	3	4	5	6	7	8	9	10	11	12	13	14	15	16	17	18	TOTAL
PAR	4	4	4	3	4	4	3	4	4	4	4	3	4	3	5	4	5	4	TOTAL
Jordan Spieth	4	3	4	3	4	4	3	3	3	4	4	3	4	2	5	4	4	4	65
Brooks Koepka	4	4	4	3	4	4	3	3	4	4	3	2	3	3	5	5	3	4	65
Matt Kuchar	4	3	4	2	3	3	3	4	3	4	4	3	4	3	5	4	5	4	65
Paul Casey	3	4	4	2	4	4	2	4	4	4	5	3	4	3	5	3	4	4	66
Charl Schwartzel	3	4	4	3	4	5	4	3	4	3	4	3	3	3	5	4	4	3	66

■ EAGLE OR BETTER ■ BIRDIES ■ BOGEYS ■ DBL BOGEYS/WORSE

SCORING SUMMARY

FIRST ROUND SCORES

Players Under Par	39
Players At Par	18
Players Over Par	99

LOW SCORES

Low First Nine
Matt Kuchar	29

Low Second Nine
Brooks Koepka	32
Rory McIlroy	32
Thomas Pieters	32
Charl Schwartzel	32

Low Round
Brooks Koepka	65
Matt Kuchar	65
Jordan Spieth	65

FIRST ROUND HOLE SUMMARY

HOLE	PAR	YARDS	EAGLES	BIRDIES	PARS	BOGEYS	D.BOGEYS	OTHER	RANK	AVERAGE
1	4	448	1	14	93	38	5	5	3	4.308
2	4	422	0	12	111	29	3	1	7	4.167
3	4	451	0	18	121	17	0	0	14	3.994
4	3	199	0	15	103	38	0	0	8	3.147
5	4	346	0	21	115	20	0	0	14	3.994
6	4	499	0	8	73	67	6	2	1	4.500
7	3	177	0	16	101	33	5	1	5	3.192
8	4	458	0	23	106	24	3	0	12	4.045
9	4	416	0	23	107	24	2	0	13	4.032
OUT	34	3,416	1	150	930	290	24	9		35.378
10	4	402	0	21	105	23	5	2	11	4.115
11	4	436	0	13	102	32	9	0	4	4.237
12	3	183	0	25	112	19	0	0	16	2.962
13	4	499	0	19	100	33	4	0	9	4.141
14	3	200	0	19	96	35	5	1	6	3.186
15	5	542	0	39	98	16	2	1	17	4.897
16	4	438	0	16	85	44	10	1	2	4.327
17	5	567	9	69	65	11	2	0	18	4.538
18	4	473	0	20	98	34	4	0	9	4.141
IN	36	3,740	9	241	861	247	41	5		36.545
TOTAL	70	7,156	10	391	1791	537	65	14		71.923

❝ *I've had my proud year and I returned the Claret Jug and now I'm just trying to get back to business again.* **❞**

—Henrik Stenson

❝ *I loved golf so much that every time a football game was cancelled, I'd be like, great, I can go practise or play golf with my friends.* **❞**

—Stuart Manley

❝ *Didn't know I was a strutter. I'm definitely playing with a bit more confidence and that's showed over the last couple of months.* **❞**

—Ian Poulter

❝ *My day was toast after that first tee shot. But I still had to play.* **❞**

—Mark O'Meara

❝ *That's a really good start. Everything was strong. I give it a nine across the board for everything — tee balls, ball-striking, short game and putting.* **❞**

—Jordan Spieth

❝ *It's a major championship. If you can't get up for that, you might as well go home.* **❞**

—Brooks Koepka

❝ *I feel like I'm in the prime of my golfing career. I feel like I certainly have as good a chance as anybody.* **❞**

—Matt Kuchar

❝ *The fans are absolutely brilliant. They did their part. I just couldn't do mine.* **❞**

—Tommy Fleetwood

Poulter's return a qualified success

Alistair Tait joins the family watching a fine opening round for 'The Postman'

Three generations of the Poulter family were involved in The 146th Open. Thirteen-year-old Luke found it hard to contain his excitement on the first day as dad Ian moved up the leaderboard. Thankfully grandad Terry was on hand to calm him down.

Call it a family affair.

Luke accompanied Ian on every step of his return to Royal Birkdale, where the Ryder Cup star finished second to Padraig Harrington in 2008. Young Luke was also there at Woburn when Ian earned his place in the Championship by coming through Final Qualifying. And he even got into the action when he

Poulter with son Luke during practice.

held up one of the "Quiet" signs as his dad prepared to putt on the eighth hole in the morning round of the 36-hole qualifier.

Luke was finding it hard to keep quiet when Ian found the fairway on the par-five 17th hole in the opening round of the Championship proper as he stood at two-under-par.

"He could eagle this and finish with a par to get to four-under," said Luke, wearing the sort of trademark tartan trousers that have helped to make Ian a household name. "And he could birdie the last, too, or he could go birdie, birdie."

That's when grandad Terry stepped in to advise a little caution. "Let's just see what happens," he said.

Luke nearly got his wish. Ian's approach shot just caught the greenside bunker and he nearly holed his shot from out of the sand. A tap-in birdie moved him to three-under-par and into a tie for the early lead with Jordan Spieth — and sent Luke scampering up the 18th fairway with grandad Terry struggling to keep up.

Poulter had opportunities to qualify for Royal Birkdale through The Open Qualifying Series. The 41-year-old Englishman competed in the French, Irish and Scottish Opens, with three exemptions into the Championship from each event. Instead, he headed to his home club of Woburn, where he has been the tournament professional since 2003, and claimed one of three spots in Final Qualifying, along with Shiv Kapur and Toby Tree.

"A lot of people have come up and said not just, 'well done for qualifying,' but 'well done for playing the qualifier,'" Poulter said. "So that is a surprise, to have so many people say that to me. It's something that you should do. If you're in a position to try and qualify for the best event in the world, then you should make the effort to go and do it. They're giving three spots away and there is a great opportunity to get into this Championship and obviously go on and hopefully win it.

"It was a special day. I think to try and qualify for this Championship is a big deal. For it to be at my home club, with huge support, was amazing. I thought there would be quite a decent gallery and several thousand turned out to watch."

Poulter drew an even larger gallery on the opening day at Royal Birkdale, when he teed-off at 8.03am in the company of Russell Knox and Alex Noren. The man nicknamed "The Postman" for his ability to deliver points in the Ryder Cup did not disappoint his fans.

Birdies at the second and fourth holes got the crowd yelling, "Come on Ian!" A bogey at the seventh, when he found a greenside bunker, was offset by a birdie at the ninth. However, the most important hole of his round came at the start of the back nine.

"A key hole for me was 10 today," Poulter said. "I didn't hit a very committed four-iron off the tee. Left myself way back in the rough, chopped it forward to 65 yards and the sand wedge shot right there

Luke with grandad Terry during qualifying at Woburn.

which I stiffed, you know, that was a good save. After birdieing nine, it would have been a shame to have let that go."

He made another good save on the 18th when he got up and down from left of the green, holing a four-foot par putt to return a three-under-par 67. The fist pump that followed was reminiscent of his 2008 celebration on the same green when he holed a 12-foot par putt he thought might win him his first major.

"It's quite nice, obviously, to go through qualifying to go out there, post a red number today, when the last time I played here in 2008 was a pretty good 69 on a tough day, as well. My last two rounds on this golf course have been good ones. And I'm pretty happy with the result today."

So was Luke. The teenager even had the satisfaction of taking £20 off John Daly's son, John Jr, in an evening, eight-hole quasi-Ryder Cup match at nearby Southport & Ainsdale.

A good day all round for the Poulter family. No wonder grandad Terry was left beaming with pride.

Spieth Enjoys a Lucky Break

By Andy Farrell

With television coverage from dawn to dusk at The Open, competitors teeing off in the afternoon have the luxury of doing research while still sitting at home.

Sometimes, however, when the weather is wreaking havoc as it did on this Friday at Royal Birkdale, it can turn into a horror show.

So Jordan Spieth found out prior to his second round of The 146th Open. "I was watching the coverage this morning and would have gladly stayed on the couch if given even par," he said. "I'd still be there right now. I'd have loved that.

"I knew it was windy and it was going to get wet — my weather app said 100 per cent by 5pm — and that was only going to make it harder. And it wasn't easy this morning. I saw Rory McIlroy was able to make some birdies early on with some really solid shots and really good control of the ball off the tee.

"But it's very difficult, one, to hit the ball like Rory and, two, when it's raining to have full con-

Jordan Spieth chips in for a dramatic par on the 10th hole.

trol of the clubface and where the ball is going. You get a little water in between the ball and the face and it could scoot way right, way left. So it was tough watching, knowing we were in for something harder."

But in golf there is no hiding place from actually going out and hitting those shots. As it turned out, Spieth got a break. Though the rain in the late afternoon and early evening was at times torrential — causing a brief 20-minute suspension in play — there were also moments when the wind, which had been blowing at more than 20mph and gusting up to 40mph for most of the day, suddenly dropped away.

"For a total of two hours today we had less wind than the guys this morning, which made a significant difference," Spieth conceded. "Fortunately we were able to take advantage of those holes and that was the key."

So whereas Matt Kuchar, from the trio of overnight American leaders, was happy to get in for a late lunch after a 71 for a four-under-par total of 136, Spieth dined on a 69 that left him with a two-stroke advantage at 134. Brooks Koepka, the third of the first-round leaders, had a 72 to fall

Richard Bland briefly tied for the lead during his 72.

Jon Rahm (74) is frustrated at his tee shot on the seventh.

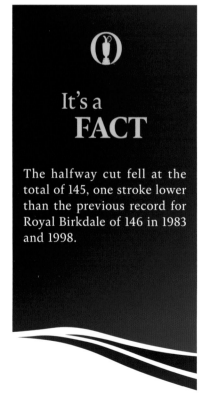

into a tie for third place with the leading home player, Ian Poulter, while Scotland's Richie Ramsay, after a 70 while playing alongside Kuchar, was in fifth place on two-under-par 138.

Spieth appeared to be sailing on his merry way after a birdie at the first hole, but he dropped his first shot of the Championship at the third and another went at the ninth. No wonder he celebrated so cheerfully after chipping in for a par at the 10th. Having been out of position after finding a bunker with his tee shot, and with his patience wearing "a bit thin" as the rain grew in intensity, Spieth delicately lofted the shot onto the green and saw it trickle down to, and into, the hole. Then came the brief break in play, and on the resumption he birdied the 11th and 12th holes. He would drop two more shots coming home but made up for them with an eagle at the 15th.

Overruling his caddie Michael Greller's suggestion to lay up, Spieth attempted to cut a three-wood out of the rough. It did not go entirely according to plan and yet worked out brilliantly. "I hit it low off the heel, which is easy to do when you're carving one

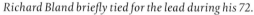

Rory McIlroy was so off line at the 15th he had to get this signpost moved.

EXCERPTS FROM THE PRESS

"To date, Jack Nicklaus is still the only player in history to collect three legs of the career grand slam before his 24th birthday; if Spieth can finish the job here, he will become the second."

—Alasdair Reid,
The Times

"Surely in a rich history that dates to 1860, The Open, played in England and Scotland, has been a stage for many lads from Glasgow. Bulle, a stocky man with a neatly trimmed beard, fits right in. He, too, is a bloke from Glasgow; Glasgow, Kentucky, that is."

—Jeff Babineau,
Golfweek

"There is always underlying trepidation with a McIlroy round at the majors — a sense of imminent drama, good or bad — so to see him fight the weather, the course and most of all himself so effectively augured well."

—Paul Hayward,
The Daily Telegraph

"Spieth and the other late starters absorbed the full fury of the one-two punch that is Royal Birkdale and Mother Nature."

—Karen Crouse,
The New York Times

Sergio Garcia reacts to his second shot on the first at the start of an eventful 69.

Charl Schwartzel seeks advice from a rules official at the fifth hole. He ended up with a double bogey and a round of 78.

like that," he explained. It came out as a low runner, ideal for links golf, and having avoided any bunkers, ran all the way up to within 18 feet of the hole. Of course, he holed the putt.

"We knew it was a bit lucky," Spieth admitted. "I got away with one there, but it was really nice to capitalise on it. I was able to knock the putt in and get to seven-under, which was a place I didn't think I'd get to starting the day. And we got in at six, so it was a very solid day, very pleased with the score."

Spieth's score was one of only eight, out of the field of 156, that were under par for the day. There had been 39 scores in the red on Thursday, but by Friday evening only nine players were under par for the Championship. They included McIlroy, after a 68, as well as American big-hitter Gary Woodland, Austin Connelly, a 20-year-old dual American-Canadian who grew up in Texas and survived a play-off in Final Qualifying to make his Open debut, and 44-year-old Richard Bland,

Gary Woodland returned a rare under-par round with a 69.

Round of the Day: Zach Johnson – 66

A 69 ensured Jamie Lovemark climbed to 10th place.

who at one point briefly tied for the lead in only his second Open appearance, 19 years after his previous outing at Birkdale ended with him missing the cut.

Not only had the wind increased from the previous day, but it had switched almost 180 degrees to come out of the southeast. Now the first hole was playing virtually downwind and was a far less stern proposition than the day before. But overall the stroke average went up by over two shots to 74.03, or effectively four-over-par.

Some players relished the different conditions. Zach Johnson, the 2015 Champion Golfer of the Year, scored the low round of the day with a 66, an improvement of nine strokes on his first-round effort. Johnson put the variation down to a number of factors, including a long session on the range on Thursday evening getting comfortable with a new driver (his old one had cracked on Tuesday), the wind switching to a direction he was more familiar with from his practice rounds, and his ability to grind out a score.

"I don't mind having my back against the wall and having to fight," he said. "That's just what I've always done." This was an Open round Johnson ranked behind only his closing 66 at St Andrews two years earlier. It also improved his position

Zach Johnson had the best score of the day with a 66.

American Brian Harman chips at the first hole.

on the leaderboard by 101 places. Sadly, Stuart Manley, the 38-year-old debutant who briefly led on Thursday morning, fell exactly 101 places in the opposite direction to miss the cut with an 81.

Playing alongside Johnson early in the morning was Sergio Garcia, who posted a 69 despite wrenching his shoulder when he took an ill-advised swish at the gorse on the fourth. While receiving ongoing treatment on the course, the Masters champion got his round back on track when he holed from off the green for an eagle-two at the fifth. Later Lee Westwood holed a full wedge shot at the same hole.

As Spieth suggested, some of the best golf to watch in the morning came from McIlroy. At the first he launched a three-wood 374 yards down the fairway, pitched close and made a birdie to get back to level par. He also birdied the third and then hit a glorious approach to five feet on the sixth to be two-under-par for the Championship or seven-under-par for his previous 18 holes. No one matched his outward 31 for the rest of the day.

Brooks Koepka stayed in contention despite a 72.

Padraig Harrington rues a missed putt at the ninth.

American Bubba Watson enjoyed a rollercoaster 72.

Richie Ramsay was top Scot on two-under-par.

Rookie Austin Connelly remained under par for two rounds.

Alfie does it for his nan

As the only one of five amateur competitors to survive the halfway cut, Alfie Plant was able to claim it was "mission accomplished" as he headed into the weekend of The 146th Open. He knew that come Sunday evening he would be standing alongside the Champion Golfer of the Year on the 18th green of Royal Birkdale as the proud recipient of the Silver Medal awarded to the leading amateur in the field.

The 25-year-old European Amateur champion dropped five strokes in his first seven holes of the second round. But an inspired fightback, cheered all the way by "Alfie's Army" of family and friends, brought him under the cut line on four-over-par.

His round of 73, including an eagle at the par-five 15th, was a splendid effort. "It's a great feeling and I'm sure it's going to get even better when it starts to sink in," he said. "The highlight was obviously the eagle. At one point, I did begin to wonder if I was going to make it but, now that I have, I can't begin to explain how good it feels."

On his bag was a printed message: "Do it for nan." It was there to remind him of his great-grandmother, Joyce, who had passed away the week previously.

"Every time I looked at the bag I got a gentle reminder. She was definitely with me this week," he said after a closing 73 for a six-over-par total of 286 and a share of 62nd place.

Spain's Rafa Cabrera Bello fell back to level par with a 73 on Friday.

A couple of important par-saves at the 10th and 11th holes kept him going, but he dropped shots at the 13th and 15th holes, after a wayward drive at the latter, though he made up for a six there with a four at the 17th. "To be under par after the way I started, I'm ecstatic with that," McIlroy said. "I set myself the target of being in a better position today than I was yesterday. Shots like the one into six and the long-iron at 17 give you a lot of confidence, and when you hole putts as I did, that really shows you are fighting for it."

Paul Casey had a 40th birthday to forget, at least while on the golf course, dropping out of contention with a 77, while Charl Schwartzel, who fleetingly tied for the lead early in the day, ended up with a 78. The only people moving up the leaderboard were still sitting at home watching on television.

Kuchar, however, embraced the battle with the elements, aided by chipping in for a birdie at the third when there was a chance he might drop his second shot in a row. A two at the fourth meant he got to six-under-par. He regained the shot that went astray at the eighth with a birdie at the 15th and only nudged his round over par by bogeying two of the last three holes.

"Conditions were really hard today," he said. "The wind was so strong and every hole it seemed to be a crosswind. What stood out to me was the 12th hole. It was playing 162 yards, wind off the left. I pulled a five-iron and had to aim 30 yards left of the pin over

Matt Kuchar (71) anxiously watches his second shot to the second green.

O'Meara does greatest walk one last time

As Mark O'Meara left the 18th green for the last time after waving farewell to The Open, he stopped to talk to officials from The R&A. His message was simple: "It's the greatest walk, it's the greatest Championship."

Having turned 60, O'Meara's exemption for winning in 1998 had expired but, alongside son Shaun as his caddie, he departed with pride intact after a 70 that was 11 strokes better than his first round. It was only the seventh time in 31 appearances he had missed the cut. "There's a little bit of life in the old dog," he said.

"I'll miss it. But I'll always watch. I know there are three other majors but I truly believe The Open is the top of the list. And the reason is

the ever-changing conditions we've witnessed the last couple of days.

"I felt the warmth of the crowd coming up the 18th hole. I'm not Tom Watson, I'm not Jack Nicklaus, I'm not Arnold Palmer. I'm just a guy who was lucky to win the Championship and be proclaimed the Champion Golfer of the Year.

"I remember playing in the final group in 1991 with Ian Baker-Finch, watching him win and being happy for my friend because he's a great guy. And seven years later when I won, after all the media stuff, I was in the clubhouse and a guy came up and put his hands on my shoulders and it was Ian Baker-Finch with a tear in his eye."

the crowd. And at the 18th I hit my driver at the bunker on the right and it ended up dead straight at the bunker — a shot penalty and a bogey to finish. I never thought the ball wouldn't move. It was quite a trying, challenging day."

At the 13th hole, Kuchar's bunker shot appeared to be stopping a foot and a half from the hole but then a gust of wind took it four feet away. Before he could hole the putt he had to back off and regroup due to another gust. But generally balls did not start rolling or oscillating on the greens due to the wind. "I think The R&A has done a nice job with the set-up," Kuchar said. "The course has some moisture, the greens can hold most of the balls."

As well as McIlroy looking more like his usual self after an injury-plagued year to date, Poulter

had the crowds excited as he clung on to the upper echelons of the leaderboard. A fist pump accompanied his putt at the ninth as he saved par from over 30 feet. He had played the entire front nine in regulation figures and then claimed a birdie-two at the 12th with a six-iron to 20 feet.

Only his second dropped shot of the Championship came on his 34th hole, or the 16th of second round, but a fine up-and-down at the last gave the 2008 runner-up a level-par 70.

"I think that round was probably better than yesterday's from the perspective of how difficult the course was playing," said the 41-year-old Englishman.

Poulter missed his first Open for a decade and

Ian Poulter agonises over his bunker shot at the eighth.

In their 99th major championships, Ernie Els made the cut…

…but Phil Mickelson missed out on the weekend this time.

a half in 2016 due to an arthritic condition in his right foot that also forced him out of the Ryder Cup. Commentating for Sky Sports at Royal Troon and acting as an assistant captain at Hazeltine National did not make up for being centre stage. He regained his PGA Tour status earlier in 2017, aided by a technicality spotted by Brian Gay's wife, and then finished tied for second at the Players Championship. That allowed Poulter the opportunity to return home and mount a bid to return to Royal Birkdale.

"This is a massive bonus for me to be in this position," he said. "I'm loving it, haven't played a major for a while and I'm pumped up. Walking up 18 was special. There are huge galleries and they were really pulling for me."

The crowds also stayed late into the evening to see home their local man, Tommy Fleetwood, who with a birdie at the 15th ensured he would be playing on the weekend for the first time at The Open. The qualifying mark fell at five-over-par 145, a record low for Birkdale, but 2008 winner

Padraig Harrington missed out by one stroke. Fellow Champion Golfers Darren Clarke (+8), Paul Lawrie (+9), Phil Mickelson (+10) and Louis Oosthuizen (+12) also missed the cut. Sadly unable to rekindle the magic of his duel with Henrik Stenson at Royal Troon, Mickelson succumbed to scores of 73 and 77, some 18 strokes higher than his 36-hole tally a year earlier.

Mickelson had scored a 63 in the first round at Royal Troon, only to be trumped by Stenson scoring the same magical number on the last day. At Erin Hills the previous month, Justin Thomas had scored the 31st major 63 during the US Open. Here at Birkdale, Thomas suffered a nine at the sixth hole before going on to miss the cut. As he tangled with the thickest and wettest of the rough on the hole, his misfortunes included the club flying out of his hands, an airshot and a drop for an unplayable lie.

Yet only weeks later Thomas would be the PGA champion and, after this Friday horror show, few could envision the record-breaking day to follow.

SECOND ROUND LEADERS

HOLE	1	2	3	4	5	6	7	8	9	10	11	12	13	14	15	16	17	18	TOTAL
PAR	4	4	4	3	4	4	3	4	4	4	4	3	4	3	5	4	5	4	
Jordan Spieth	3	4	5	3	4	4	3	4	5	4	3	2	4	4	3	5	5	4	69-134
Matt Kuchar	4	5	3	2	4	4	3	5	4	4	4	3	4	3	5	4	5	5	71-136
Ian Poulter	4	4	4	3	4	4	3	4	4	4	4	2	4	3	5	5	5	4	70-137
Brooks Koepka	4	4	4	3	4	5	3	4	4	4	4	3	5	3	5	4	5	4	72-137
Richie Ramsay	4	4	4	3	4	4	3	4	4	4	4	3	5	3	5	4	4	4	70-138
Austin Connelly	4	4	4	3	4	4	3	4	4	4	3	5	4	5	4	4	5	5	72-139
Rory McIlroy	3	4	3	3	4	3	3	4	4	4	4	3	5	3	6	4	4	4	68-139
Gary Woodland	4	4	4	3	2	5	4	4	4	3	4	3	5	3	4	4	5	4	69-139
Richard Bland	4	3	4	2	4	5	3	5	4	4	4	3	6	2	6	4	5	4	72-139

■ EAGLE OR BETTER ■ BIRDIES ■ BOGEYS ■ DBL BOGEYS/WORSE

SCORING SUMMARY

SECOND ROUND SCORES

Players Under Par	8
Players At Par	7
Players Over Par	141

LOW SCORES

Low First Nine
Rory McIlroy — 31

Low Second Nine
Kevin Kisner — 32

Low Round
Zach Johnson — 66

SECOND ROUND HOLE SUMMARY

HOLE	PAR	YARDS	EAGLES	BIRDIES	PARS	BOGEYS	D.BOGEYS	OTHER	RANK	AVERAGE
1	4	448	0	16	116	23	1	0	16	4.058
2	4	422	0	13	111	30	1	1	12	4.141
3	4	451	0	5	100	46	4	1	5	4.333
4	3	199	0	14	113	25	3	1	14	3.128
5	4	346	3	21	121	9	2	0	17	3.910
6	4	499	0	6	71	66	10	3	2	4.583
7	3	177	0	8	93	50	5	0	5	3.333
8	4	458	0	3	97	53	3	0	4	4.359
9	4	416	0	6	106	37	6	1	8	4.295
OUT	34	3,416	3	92	928	339	35	7		36.141
10	4	402	0	23	92	36	5	0	11	4.147
11	4	436	0	14	101	34	7	0	10	4.218
12	3	183	0	20	72	54	6	4	3	3.378
13	4	499	0	0	68	69	17	2	1	4.705
14	3	200	0	8	101	43	4	0	9	3.276
15	5	542	6	67	67	14	2	0	18	4.609
16	4	438	0	22	102	28	4	0	15	4.090
17	5	567	2	26	88	31	6	3	12	5.141
18	4	473	1	4	99	48	4	0	7	4.321
IN	36	3,740	9	184	790	357	55	9		37.885
TOTAL	70	7,156	12	276	1,718	696	90	16		74.026

Seeking the invincible stare

Lewine Mair keeps an eye on all the shuffling and strutting on view at The Open

For every golf fanatic who is concerned with the position of a player's club at the top of the swing, there is another who is more intent on studying his or her body language.

Matt Kuchar, for instance, made for endless debate at The Open. He was never less than a smiling and sportsmanlike presence, yet the picture which will remain is of a man who, at six feet four inches, was shuffling uncomfortably around in bunkers which were way too small for him. It was as if someone needed to suggest that he should pick on hazards which made for a better fit.

Had that applied, this endlessly popular American could well have improved on his sand saves

statistics — four out of eight as opposed, say, to Rory McIlroy's eight out of nine.

McIlroy's body language, to give a very different example, left people with the impression that there was more than one of him.

For the first six holes on Thursday, in which he was five-over-par, this four-time major winner was shaking his head and looking utterly desolate. Yet for the holes which followed, he was back with his old jaunty stride and it was catching.

The fans stopped moping and the feel-good factor was everywhere apparent as their player birdied and bounced his way to a 71. Mind you, to give credit where credit was due, most of that massed

Happiness was down to JP Fitzgerald, McIlroy's loyal and long-time caddie.

Plenty of caddies think twice about delivering home truths for fear of losing their jobs but Fitzgerald, who did in fact part company with his boss just over a week later, was in no mood to tread carefully. He said precisely what was on his mind. "You're Rory McIlroy. What the hell are you doing?"

McIlroy (left) mumbled a grudging, "whatever," but he would later concede just how much that rebuke did for him: "It helped, it definitely helped." By the end of the week, he was five-under-par as opposed to five-over and picking up the £366,048 prize-money attached to a share of fourth place.

Ian Poulter, meantime, was a ball of fire from the start. The Englishman (below) had missed most of 2016 through injury and he was raring to be let loose in a major championship context. Thomas Bjørn, the 2018 Ryder Cup captain, was one of the first to comment on the return of Poulter's Ryder Cup "strut," while he had even tipped

him as a possible winner. (Poulter, incidentally, was alone in denying that he was "a strutter.")

The strutting was by no means the only thing to set Poulter apart at Royal Birkdale. When he missed the 18th green with his second shot on the third day, the pale fury on his face was allied to a still more telling barometer of his inner feelings. As he proceeded down the fairway, he gripped his club at either end and arched it, rainbow-like, across his chest. Luckily for him, it did not break.

Sergio Garcia was not so lucky when, in a fit of

club, like Poulter's, survived the attack, but Garcia's shoulder did not. The Spaniard knew at once that he had done it a mischief and the injury played up from time to time until the end of the Championship.

This, perhaps, was why the 2017 Masters champion was asked to name the player with the best body language in golf. He chose Dustin Johnson, but only after delivering the deliciously impish line "You mean the best body language after me?"

Body language can include a stare which belongs to the few and the very few. Jack Nicklaus had it. Poulter has it. As does Tiger Woods, Dottie Pepper, Graeme McDowell (on occasion) and, as we were reminded over the closing holes at Birkdale, Jordan Spieth (above). Pete Cowen, who coaches so many of the stars, has described the stare as "a state which says, 'Don't touch me, I'm invincible."

If officials were to inform any of the above starers that a man-eating tiger was approaching, they would not want to know. Yet if the same information was relayed to a Mark O'Meara, a Branden Grace or a Kuchar, the chances are that each member of that little group would be more inclined to ask if there was anything he could do to help.

For the most part, body language is not something which can easily be taught. However, there is a case for suggesting that it can be inherited.

By all accounts, there are those at Royal Troon who swear that Colin Montgomerie, when his shoulders slump a good six inches in the wake of a bogey, is merely mirroring the body language of

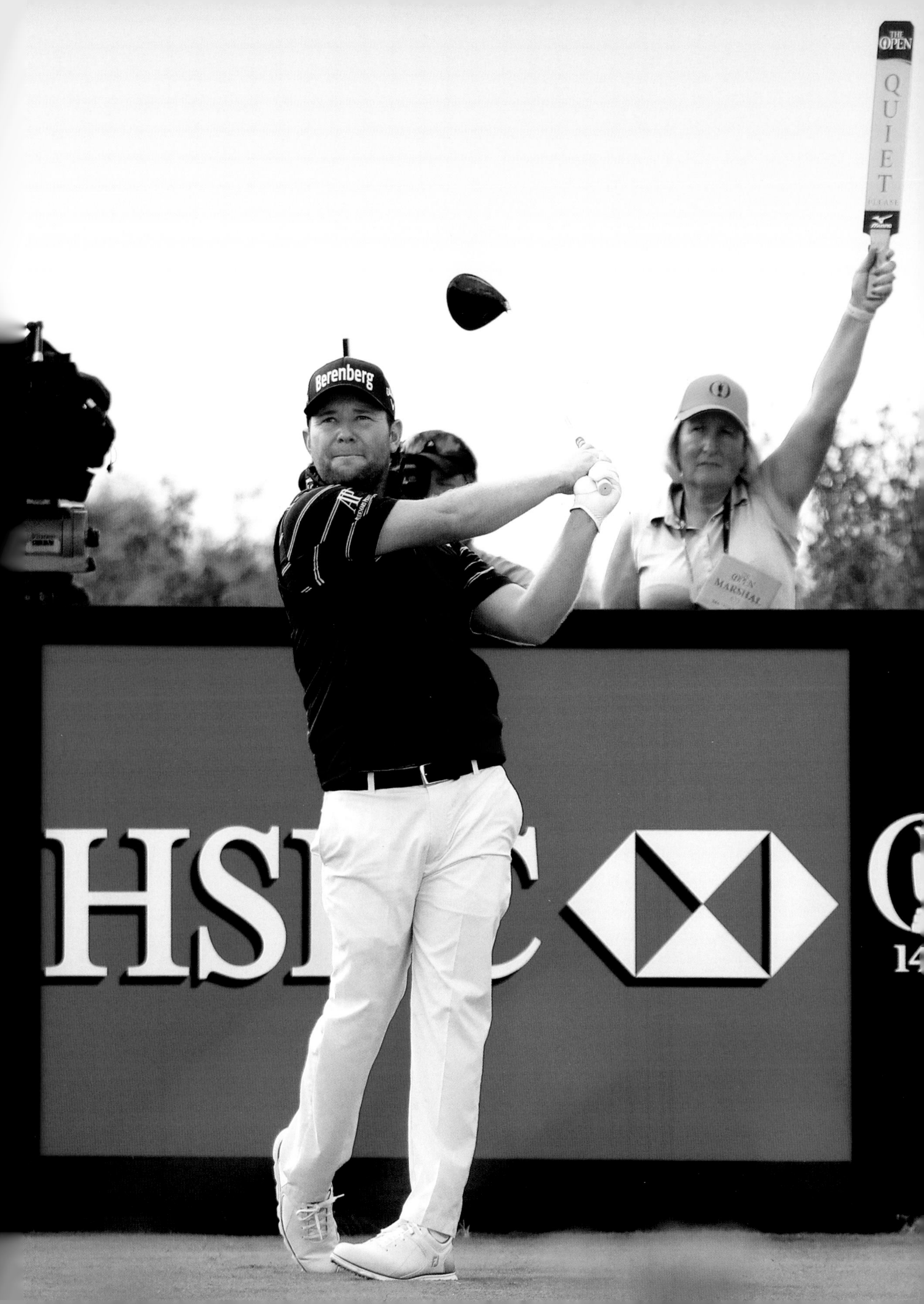
THE OPEN
QUIET
PLEASE
Berenberg
MARSHAL

THIRD ROUND
22 July 2017

Birkdale Graced With Historic 62

By Andy Farrell

This was a day that had threatened to arrive many times before. And everyone seemed to know it. Royal Birkdale had shown its beastly side over the opening two days of The 146th Open, but the course was damp after an overnight soaking, the wind had disappeared and the sun was out. It was links golfing heaven.

Shaun Norris, out with a marker in the first game of the day, scored 65. "The course is out there to take on," he said. Jason Day, the former world number one who spent most of Friday afternoon watching *The Expendables 2* and eating ice cream in expectation of missing the cut, also had a 65, as did his Australian compatriot Scott Hend. "I definitely think there is a good opportunity to shoot 62 out there today," Day said.

Tommy Fleetwood, out early with Justin Rose

Branden Grace tees off at the 17th in his historic round.

and followed by a huge gallery again, was among those who scored 66. "There's no reason why any of us can't do it," he said. "You're always trying to force every last ounce out of every round." Paul Casey added: "There was talk that 62 could be on. My coach, Peter Kostis, suggested, 'Why don't you do it?'" The Englishman could not quite manage it, but at least his 67 was 10 better than his score the previous day.

In his new job as an on-course commentator for NBC/Golf Channel, Jim "Bones" Mackay pronounced that the men's major championship record of 63, first achieved by one of his new colleagues, Johnny Miller, at the 1973 US Open, could fall. A year earlier Bones had fallen onto the 18th green at Royal Troon in disbelief at a putt for a 62 from his former boss, Phil Mickelson, lipping out. Mickelson reasoned he had been cursed by the golfing gods.

Not Branden Grace. Apparently a curse you are unaware of cannot hurt you. "I didn't know what was going on on 18," the South African insisted. "I promise you." He was the only one who did not.

"I honestly didn't," Grace added. "I was so in the zone of playing, hole after hole. I knew I was

A 67 for Rafa Cabrera Bello.

Leaders Jordan Spieth and Matt Kuchar enjoyed the good scoring conditions.

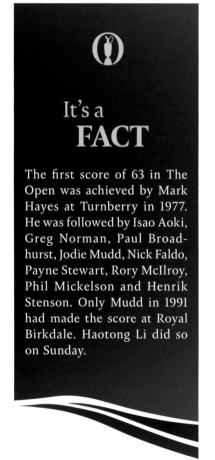

It's a FACT

The first score of 63 in The Open was achieved by Mark Hayes at Turnberry in 1977. He was followed by Isao Aoki, Greg Norman, Paul Broadhurst, Jodie Mudd, Nick Faldo, Payne Stewart, Rory McIlroy, Phil Mickelson and Henrik Stenson. Only Mudd in 1991 had made the score at Royal Birkdale. Haotong Li did so on Sunday.

obviously playing really well, and making the turn in five-under-par was pretty special. And I thought if I could make a couple more on the back nine, then it's going to be a great score. I had no idea that 62 was obviously the lowest ever."

His caddie, Zack Rasego, had done the maths. Three birdies coming home, added to the five going out, along with no bogeys, meant an eight-under-par effort on a par-70 layout and that gave rise to a historic first sighting of the mythical 62. From four-over-par and a tie for 45th place, Grace was now tied for second place alongside Matt Kuchar, two behind overnight leader Jordan Spieth.

By the end of the day's play, Grace was in fifth place, tied with Hideki Matsuyama, seven off the lead. He was only one behind Brooks Koepka and Austin Connelly, but Spieth and Kuchar had separated themselves from the rest at 11-under-par and eight-under-par respectively.

History and records were the last thing on Grace's mind when he teed-off at 11.25 accompanied by Jason Dufner, himself a member of the 63 club. Grace knows how to go low and scored a 12-under-par 60 at Kingsbarns in winning the Alfred Dunhill Links Championship in 2012. But he had only one aim starting his third round here. "I was concentrating on getting myself back into this tournament," he said, "and giving myself a chance tomorrow.

"It was nice to start off with a birdie on the first, made a nice

Local favourite Tommy Fleetwood and Olympic gold medallist Justin Rose entertain a huge gallery at the seventh.

Early starters Shaun Norris and Jason Day showed what might be possible with rounds of 65.

Stenson and Johnson on the move

With Henrik Stenson's record-breaking victory at Royal Troon in 2016, when he held Phil Mickelson at bay with a final round of 63, still fresh in the memory and Dustin Johnson, the 2016 US Open champion, at the top of the world rankings, both were considered potential winners at the start of Open week.

While Stenson's form had dipped in 2017, Johnson's only stalled after he fell down stairs on the eve of the Masters and had to withdraw because of a back injury. In the first two rounds at Royal Birkdale, both players trod water. Stenson (above left) had rounds of 69 and 73, while Johnson (above right) had scores of 71 and 72 and trailed Jordan Spieth, the leader, by nine strokes.

suddenly had the leaders in their sights in what were considerably improved conditions. It says something about Johnson's reputation that no sooner had Branden Grace broken the all-time major record with a round of 62, the South African was musing that the American might be about to better it.

Johnson had gone to the turn in 30, was six-under-par through 15 holes, and needed to pick up two more strokes to equal Grace's record. It was not to be. Johnson had three pars to finish in a bogey-free round of 64 and ended the day tied for seventh alongside Stenson, who had a 65.

They would be playing together on the final day but closing the gap on Spieth proved beyond ever

A 69 for Alex Noren.

Hideki Matsuyama missed his putt at the last but signed for a 66.

putt. It always gives you some momentum and some confidence heading into the round. And then I just played flawless golf. I think I missed two fairways and two greens all day. The putter was hot. I missed a couple of shortish ones but made a couple of bombs, which was nice."

Grace missed from eight feet on the third green — missing other good chances at the 13th and 15th holes — but made one of those bombs, from 35 feet, at the fourth. The tee at the fifth was moved up so the par four was playing only 287 yards. Rickie Fowler had the shortest possible tap-in for an eagle-two, having been tantalisingly close to a rare hole-in-one albatross. Grace drove the green and two-putted for a three.

The next two birdies came at the eighth, from 25 feet, and the ninth, from 12 feet to tie Kuchar's 29 from the first day. Four pars followed. Another bomb from 34 feet fell at the short 14th, and at six-under-par with two par fives to come, the "62 watch" was firmly on. He parred the 15th but made up for it by holing from 28 feet at the 16th. Then he found the green at the 17th with a three-iron and two-putted to go eight-under-par for the day.

Playing his approach to the last with a wedge,

Kuchar whips his driver off the eighth tee.

62 watch: Grace holes a putt from 28 feet at the 16th green for his seventh birdie of the day.

Grace hits his approach to the 18th unaware of the history he is about to make.

Round of the Day: **Branden Grace – 62**

	OFFICIAL SCORECARD THE 146TH OPEN ROYAL BIRKDALE		

Branden GRACE
Game 13
Saturday 22 July at 11.25 am

FOR R&A USE ONLY 13.1		ROUND 3
36 HOLE TOTAL	144	54 HOLE TOTAL
THIS ROUND	62	206
54 HOLE TOTAL	206	

VERIFIED *bmg*

ROUND 3

Hole	1	2	3	4	5	6	7	8	9	Out	10	11	12	13	14	15	16	17	18	In	Total
Yards	448	422	451	199	346	499	177	458	416	3416	402	436	183	499	200	542	438	567	473	3740	7156
Par	4	4	4	3	4	4	3	4	4	34	4	4	3	4	3	5	4	5	4	36	70
Score	3	4	4	2	3	4	3	5	3	29	4	4	3	4	2	5	3	4	4	33	62

Signature of Marker

Signature of Competitor
Branden Grace

the ball jumped out of the semi-rough and ran to the back of the green. "My whole thing on the 18th was trying just not to make bogey," Grace said. "I wanted to finish strong. You always feel so bad making a bogey on the last hole, especially after a good day like that."

If the curse was going to strike, it would be now. But Grace hit a superb lag putt to just outside two feet from the hole. With all due care and attention, the par putt found the hole. "That's when Zack came up and said, 'You're in the history books.' And I said, 'What are you talking about?'

"Obviously, he knew but he never said anything until I made the putt, so good on him. Now it makes it even more special. And even though I've not always finished great at The Open, it's an event that

Rory McIlroy drives at the 15th, where he made a birdie, but otherwise squandered a fine start.

A fine 66 for England's Ross Fisher.

I've always enjoyed playing in. What a special place to get myself in the history books."

Only one of the 10 rounds of 63 in The Open had been at Birkdale, by Jodie Mudd in 1991. Suddenly, another 62 or even a 61 was a possibility with Dustin Johnson five-under-par after 10 holes. Yet the world number one only grabbed one more birdie and so finished with a 64 to tie for seventh place. On the same three-under-par mark was Henrik Stenson, making a valiant defence of his title with a 65.

The home challenge was stuck on two-under-par. Ross Fisher got there with a 66 and Richie Ramsay stayed there after his second successive 70. But Ian Poulter's campaign stalled with a 71, containing five bogeys when he had recorded only two over the first two days. His was one of only 19 scores over par. The 43 scores in the 60s, by contrast, was a new high for the third round of The Open since records began in 1946.

At six-under-par for the round playing the 16th, Dustin Johnson had a chance to match Grace but settled for a 64.

Sadly for Richie Ramsay there was no pot of gold, nor a Claret Jug, at the end of this rainbow.

Brooks Koepka hits his tee shot at the 14th under dark skies.

McIlroy's 69 was one of them, but the round promised so much more after he was three-under-par for the first five holes. It was the second day in a row he had made a fine start, but this time he could not sustain it, in particular lapsing to a double-bogey-six at the 10th after a poor tee shot and twice finding bunkers.

It was a day to remember, however, for Connelly, a 20-year-old rookie on the European Tour. He birdied the first, holed out from the fairway for an eagle-two at the second and birdied his last two holes for a 66. A week previously he had finished down the field at a Challenge Tour event in Sardinia. The next day he would be playing alongside the US Open champion Koepka in the penultimate game of the day.

Koepka posted a 68, but that made no impression on Saturday's final pairing of Spieth and Kuchar. For the second time in the week, Spieth returned a bogey-free 65, while Kuchar's 66 meant he fell a further stroke behind. Spieth's 54-hole total of

Young Austin introduces himself

When Austin Connelly powered his approach at the second into the hole for an eagle-two, after a birdie at the first, the 20-year-old was just two strokes off the lead. "It was an incredible rush," he said. "The crowd went crazy. I had 145 yards into the wind off the right and hit a nine-iron as flush as I could hit it."

It was quite a way to introduce himself to the golfing public. The Open rookie, a 500-1 shot who played amateur golf for Canada due to his father's nationality, turned professional after leaving high school and spent 2017 as an international man of mystery playing on the lower reaches of the European and Challenge Tours. Until now the highlight was making a birdie at the first extra

hole of a four-way play-off for one spot in Final Qualifying at Royal Cinque Ports.

Plotting his way around a links came naturally to a player who loves competing in the wind. His third-round 66 left him tied for third place, albeit six behind his friend Jordan Spieth.

"His round today was tremendous," Spieth said. "He's got a great head. He's got a killer instinct." Connelly drifted out to 14th place on Sunday but, with Spieth's victory, he could say he has two friends who are Champion Golfers of the Year. He often plays golf with Todd Hamilton and was watching on television as a seven-year-old when Hamilton won at Royal Troon in 2004.

Kuchar got within one of Spieth on the inward nine but ended up trailing his compatriot by three.

199 was one stroke off The Open record but six better than the previous best for Royal Birkdale, set by Tom Watson in 1983.

With Kuchar birdieing the second and hitting close at the third, which became another birdie, Spieth was relieved to get into the duel at the same hole with an eight-iron to little more than six inches. Both players were out in 31, Spieth holing from 12 feet at the seventh and then matching Kuchar's three at the eighth.

A series of pars followed for both players as the skies darkened. A storm threatened, but what rain ensued did not hinder the see-sawing action. From the short 14th, Kuchar had three birdies and a double-bogey, while Spieth birdied the 15th but only after holing a decent second putt to avoid being tied. Having got within one, Kuchar took a six at the 16th by visiting a bunker and then three-putting to fall three behind for the first time.

Both found the same greenside bunker at the 17th, but Kuchar hit out close to make a four while Spieth had to settle for a par. When Kuchar hit his approach close at the last, it looked as if the lead might be down to one again. Spieth's second shot only just avoided the right-hand bunker but

did find the putting surface. Spieth was reaching for his map of the green to study his putt only to realise the crowd was acclaiming the two gladiators.

Spieth explained: "I started to take out my book, but I'm like, I can't. This is not worthy of this. Everyone is giving us an ovation and it's a time to appreciate that, enjoy the walk, but also to say 'thank you' for the support that these crowds give us.

"I think these crowds are second to none. They're the most educated golf fans. And the 18th hole walk is a really, really special thing to do, whether it's Monday in a practice round or it's Saturday or Sunday afternoon. Matt came over and said, 'This is a cool moment, let's enjoy it.' I was already appreciating it but it was a cool thing for him to do. I really enjoy playing golf with him."

Rising to the occasion is what Spieth does, so it was no surprise when he holed his putt from 15 feet for a three. Kuchar was certainly not surprised, but when he failed to convert from inside 10 feet it was a blow to the challenger. He would start Sunday three behind. "That's expected with Jordan," Kuchar said. "I had a good feeling about my putt. If Jordan made his, I was going to make

"Polite applause fits Ian Poulter as badly as a sober suit, but that was his accompaniment as he laboured around Royal Birkdale yesterday in fits and starts of birdies and bogeys and his longed-for challenge for The Open ebbed slowly and sadly away."
—Oliver Holt,
The Mail on Sunday

"No one has ever posted all four rounds in the 60s at Birkdale. In a week when one major record has been ripped up by Branden Grace, who would be surprised if Spieth was to rewrite Birkdale's history too?"
—Euan McLean,
Sunday Mail

"It would be fitting if he picked up the third leg of the career grand slam at a place that puts so much emphasis on great iron play, because whether you realise it or not, in the past year, Spieth has become the best iron player on tour."
—Kevin Van Valkenburg, ESPN

"A course that was virtually unplayable in the wind and rain of Friday afternoon was made to look like a pitch-and-putt in the local park by Branden Grace yesterday."
—Andrew Longmore,
The Sunday Times

146TH ROYAL BIRKDALE

Austin Connelly celebrates a birdie at the 18th and a share of third place.

it on top, but mine slid by the edge. That's part of the game. It was a fun round of golf. I never felt I was trying to beat Jordan, just put on the best show you can against the golf course. But it was certainly a fun back and forth."

Spieth had set out with the aim of scoring a 66, two-under-par for each half, so the birdie at the 18th was a bonus. The low scoring all day, however, had changed his thinking at the start of the round. "Recognising that it was a very favourable day for scoring made it pretty mentally tough," he said. "When you're leading you might play a little safer, par being a good score, but it was a day when you had to be aggressive. But it was a really solid round and I'm extremely pleased."

By the age of 23, Spieth already had plenty of experience of leading major championships, both good and bad. He could not avoid a question about the 2016 Masters, when he imploded at the 12th hole. "It was a humbling experience that I thought could serve me well going forward," he said.

"If I don't win tomorrow, it has nothing to do with it. If I do win tomorrow, it has nothing to do with it. You're always learning. The next 18-20 hours are about being very positive and staying focused. It's not going to get any easier. Tomorrow will be emotionally draining and it'll be important to stay neutral in the head."

Easier said than done, as they say, and as Spieth was reminded on the final day.

Kuchar and Spieth share the applause of the gallery as they walk up the 18th.

THIRD ROUND LEADERS

HOLE	1	2	3	4	5	6	7	8	9	10	11	12	13	14	15	16	17	18	TOTAL
PAR	4	4	4	3	4	4	3	4	4	4	4	3	4	3	5	4	5	4	TOTAL
Jordan Spieth	4	4	3	3	4	4	2	3	4	4	4	3	4	3	4	4	5	3	65-199
Matt Kuchar	4	3	3	4	3	4	3	4	4	4	3	4	2	4	6	4	4		66-202
Austin Connelly	3	2	5	3	4	4	3	5	3	4	4	4	3	4	5	4	4	3	66-205
Brooks Koepka	5	4	3	2	3	4	4	3	4	4	4	3	5	3	4	4	4	5	68-205
Branden Grace	3	4	4	2	3	4	3	3	3	4	4	3	4	2	5	3	4	4	62-206
Hideki Matsuyama	4	4	4	4	3	3	2	4	4	4	4	3	4	2	5	4	4	4	66-206

■ EAGLE OR BETTER ■ BIRDIES ■ BOGEYS ■ DBL BOGEYS/WORSE

SCORING SUMMARY

THIRD ROUND SCORES

Players Under Par	43
Players At Par	15
Players Over Par	19

LOW SCORES

Low First Nine
Branden Grace — 29

Low Second Nine
Scott Hend — 31

Low Round
Branden Grace — 62

THIRD ROUND HOLE SUMMARY

HOLE	PAR	YARDS	EAGLES	BIRDIES	PARS	BOGEYS	D.BOGEYS	OTHER	RANK	AVERAGE
1	4	448	0	15	46	15	1	0	8	4.026
2	4	422	1	12	58	6	0	0	13	3.896
3	4	451	0	10	58	8	1	0	9	4.000
4	3	199	0	10	55	11	1	0	7	3.039
5	4	346	4	29	39	4	1	0	17	3.597
6	4	499	0	7	52	18	0	0	2	4.143
7	3	177	0	13	59	5	0	0	13	2.896
8	4	458	0	20	43	10	2	2	9	4.000
9	4	416	0	16	51	8	2	0	12	3.948
OUT	34	3,416	5	132	461	85	8	2		33.545
10	4	402	0	9	61	6	1	0	11	3.987
11	4	436	0	5	60	12	0	0	5	4.091
12	3	183	0	4	58	12	3	0	1	3.182
13	4	499	0	7	55	14	1	0	3	4.117
14	3	200	0	11	65	1	0	0	15	2.870
15	5	542	2	41	31	3	0	0	18	4.455
16	4	438	0	9	53	13	2	0	4	4.104
17	5	567	3	33	34	5	2	0	16	4.610
18	4	473	0	9	54	14	0	0	6	4.065
IN	36	3,740	5	128	471	80	9	0		35.481
TOTAL	70	7,156	10	260	932	165	17	2		69.026

" Sooner or later someone is going to break 62. But hopefully it takes a while. "
—Branden Grace

" It was always going to be a great sort of crowd when it was me and Justin — me being the local boy and him being Justin Rose. "
—Tommy Fleetwood

" I believed when I turned professional that I was going to rise and be able to play with the best in the world. And it's just nice to have that confirmed. "
—Austin Connelly

" Walking up the 18th, the last group Saturday of The Open, having the stands and the people cheer, it's completely unique. "
—Matt Kuchar

" Dustin always has a swagger. It's just a Dustin swagger. It's not more or less. It's the same swagger if it's a double-bogey as it is from an eagle. And that's what's really cool about Dustin Johnson. "
—Paul Casey

" All the girls out there, I end up with a Daisy. What's the chances? "
—Alfie Plant

" Today was an opportunity lost to get right in the mix going into tomorrow. "
—Rory McIlroy

" I know I needed to shoot low today, but I don't ever say, 'I'm going to shoot 64.' I just try to shoot as low as I can. "
—Dustin Johnson

Amazing Grace's record 62

Art Spander witnesses a historic round 44 years after Miller's original 63

It was the round we had waited for, the score that reminded us how easy golf could seem while at the same time reminding us how difficult golf had been. It was the 62 by Branden Grace in The 146th Open. It also was the 63 by Johnny Miller in the 1973 US Open. And, as fate and fable would dictate, I was there for both.

There at Oakmont when in the last round Miller, starting six shots back, overtook Arnold Palmer, the hometown guy, and several others — a round so unexpected that Miller's wife, Linda, had stayed back in the room to pack and was rushed to the course just before the end.

There at Royal Birkdale when in the third round Grace, almost oblivious to his accomplishment, unprecedented in men's major championships, moved up from 45th place to a tie for fifth and yet failed to

grasp what he had done until caddie Zack Rasego told him, "You're in the history books."

And in the broadcast booth for America's NBC television was Miller, a man who 44 years earlier made his own history — "Miller's Miracle" was the headline on the cover of the US weekly *Sports Illustrated* — and in a few hours, the time taken for Grace's round, had lost his record.

A month ahead of Grace, in the US Open at Erin Hills, Justin Thomas shot the 31st major 63, but because the course played to a par 72, not 70 as at Oakmont or Royal Birkdale, and he was lower in relation to par, nine-under, some judged that more impressive. Subjectivity about a very objective sport.

"It ain't how, it's how many," remains the essential truism in golf. Lloyd Mangrum's 64 at the 1940 Masters was the benchmark in the majors. Until Miller's

63 in the 1973 US Open. Until Grace's 62 in the 2017 Open. If the greens were soft, if The R&A's set-up was less challenging — even Grace said par was about 67 — so? Nobody else shot 62, did they? End of debate.

Miller was 26 in 1973, two years earlier having led the Masters with three holes to play. Grace was 29 in 2017, having two years earlier been tied for the lead of the US Open with three holes to play. Each then had given notice of what might be, not that a record score ever is predictable.

The first two days at Oakmont, Miller was grouped with Palmer and in contention. In the third round Miller left his yardage book in the room and shot 76. He was out of it. In 12th place, six shots behind the co-leaders, one of whom was the legendary Arnie. Then Miller opened his final round with four straight birdies. He would hit all 18 greens but three-putt the eighth hole for a bogey.

What I remember is Arnold Palmer, looking at one of the leaderboards and gawking. "Who the hell is that five-under?" he asked after the turn.

Grace was blissfully ignorant of how he was progressing, thinking, as golfers are advised, just about the moment, about the next shot. "I was just in the zone, taking it hole by hole," was his comment.

Miller, an uninhibited Californian, was fully aware of how he stood and delightfully candid, a quality

ROUND THREE
GAME No. 13

SATURDAY 22 JULY 2017

THE OPEN
146TH ROYAL BIRKDALE

HOLE	YARDS	PAR	SCORE	COMMENTS
COMPETITOR: BRANDEN GRACE		SCORE 62	PREVIOUS SCORE ROUND 3	TOTAL
1	448	4	(3)	DRIVER, 127 yds LEFT TO HOLE, GAP WEDGE TO 16ft
2	422	4	4	DRIVER, 130 yds TO HOLE, GAP WEDGE, 2-PUTT PAR
3	451	4	4	DRIVER, 158 yds TO HOLE, 9 IRON TO 8ft
4	199	3	(2)	8-IRON, 176 yds TO HOLE, 35ft PUTT
5	346	4	(3)	DRIVER, 283 yds TO GREEN, 2 PUTT BIRDIE FROM 25ft
6	499	4	4	DRIVER, 218 yds TO HOLE, 3-IRON, 2-PUTT PAR
7	177	3	3	9-IRON - 157 yds TO HOLE, 2 PUTTS FROM 16ft
8	458	4	(3)	DRIVER, 158 yds TO HOLE, 9-IRON TO 25ft
9	416	4	(3)	DRIVER, 129 yds TO HOLE, GAP WEDGE TO 12ft
OUT	3416	34	29	
10	402	4	4	5-IRON, 161 yds TO HOLE, 9-IRON SHORT OF GREEN, 2 PUTTS
11	436	4	4	DRIVER, 173 yds TO HOLE, 7-IRON, 2 PUTT
12	183	3	3	6-IRON, 184 yds TO HOLE, 2 PUTTS FROM 15ft
13	499	4	4	DRIVER, 180 yds TO HOLE, 2 PUTT FROM 11ft
14	200	3	(2)	9-IRON, 164 yds TO HOLE, 34ft BIRDIE PUTT
15	542	5	5	DRIVER, 210 yds TO HOLE, 2-IRON MISSED GREEN SHORT LEFT, CHIP TO 7ft
16	438	4	(3)	DRIVER, 162 yds TO HOLE, 9 IRON, 28ft BIRDIE PUTT
17	567	5	(4)	DRIVER, 239 yds TO HOLE, 3-IRON, 2 PUTTS FROM 26ft
18	473	4	4	DRIVER, 165 yds TO HOLE, 2 PUTT OVER GREEN, 2 PUTTS FOR PAR
IN	3740	36	33	
TOTAL	7156	70	62	

less so by pro golfers when he says about them the negative things he once said about himself.

"After I birdied the third hole," Miller told us, "I said to myself, 'Son of a gun, I'm even par.' And I thought, 'Well, maybe I've got a chance to get back in the tournament!' But when I birdied the fourth I got a little tight. I almost gagged on a couple of putts at the seventh and eighth but the easy birdie at nine calmed me down."

Grace needed no calming. On the contrary. Hey, Branden, somebody joked, you missed a day of beautiful golf. "I knew I was playing really well," Grace did admit, "and making the turn in five-under was pretty special. I thought if I could make a couple more on the back nine it was going to be a great score. I had no idea that 62 was the lowest ever."

A year earlier, on the first day at Royal Troon, Phil Mickelson was 18 feet away from a birdie and a 62 but the ball spun out. Playing with Mickelson was Ernie Els, who said "I don't know how that putt didn't go in." Twelve months later, Els marvelled at his fellow South African: "I'm really proud of him. Today it was on, but you still have to hit the shots and make the putts."

And from behind the glass of the broadcast booth, Miller told an American audience, "The course was set up really, really easy today, folks, but still a heck of record."

As was Miller's, the one I watched and the one

FOURTH ROUND
23 July 2017

Spieth Puts on a Show

By Andy Farrell

It was never going to be easy, but Jordan Spieth could hardly have imagined how hard it would be. Royal Birkdale rarely lacks for drama and the Texan was at the heart of it as The 146th Open climaxed in a thrilling fashion.

"Boy, this was eventful," he marvelled. "As I say, 17 pars and a birdie would have been fine, too. But there are a lot of roads to get there. Today took as much out of me as any day that I've ever played golf."

Spieth started the day with a three-stroke lead and won by the same margin — a summation that in no way does justice to the spectacular finale witnessed by record crowds, the growing greatness of Spieth as a competitive golfer, or the sorrow inflicted on Matt Kuchar, a gentleman who did everything within his command to outwit the ancient links but was thwarted by a victor of rare audacity.

Jordan Spieth celebrates his birdie at the 16th hole.

Having frittered away his lead, Spieth somehow salvaged an extraordinary bogey at the epic 13th hole to fall only one behind. Then he did what only one of the special ones can do and finished birdie-eagle-birdie-birdie-par. "It was impressive stuff when a guy does something like that," Kuchar said. "All you can really do is sit back, tip your cap and say, 'well done.' It was certainly a show he put on."

In becoming the Champion Golfer of the Year for 2017, Spieth won his third major title and, more than that, his third different major championship to join only Jack Nicklaus in claiming a third leg of the grand slam before the age of 24. Spieth's birthday followed four days later and the Claret Jug, taken into possession with an eloquent speech on the Sunday evening at Birkdale, was a treasured guest at the party.

Spieth shared the lead on the first day with Kuchar and Brooks Koepka, and then held it outright for the rest of the Championship. So he did not quite join the seven players who have led on their own throughout, including Bobby Jones in 1927, Tiger Woods in 2005 and Rory McIlroy in 2014. But he did set a new winning total for Birkdale of 268 and became the first player to score four rounds

Rory McIlroy hits a bunker shot at the 15th hole in his final round of three-under-par 67.

Rafa Cabrera Bello closed with a 68 to share fourth place with McIlroy.

in the 60s at the famous links, and the fifth Champion Golfer of the Year to do so anywhere.

Yet while such feats are building a picture of Spieth's place in the very highest ranks of the game, it was how he won at Birkdale that will forever be remembered. In his previous tournament, the Travelers Championship in the US, he had led after every round but closed shakily and only won courtesy of an outrageous hole-out from a bunker at the first extra hole.

Front-running again here proved even more stressful. It looked at one point as if he would do well to get into a play-off, not just with Kuchar but China's Haotong Li. The 21-year-old Open debutant started the day 12 strokes off the lead but, just as the leaders were struggling at the start of their rounds, he birdied the last four holes for a 63. It was no longer a record score, thanks to Branden Grace's 62 the previous day, but it elevated Li to third on the leaderboard and set the clubhouse target at six-under-par 274.

Though there were times in the day when either Kuchar or Spieth fell to seven-under-par, neither fell into a tie with the Chinese player. But Li's superb effort secured him third place, in only his second major appearance, and a spot in the 2018 Masters.

As it turned out, Spieth and Kuchar in the last game of the day

Li's dream Open debut

On being told that his exceptional score of 63 in the final round of The Open — and subsequent climb to third on the leaderboard — had secured him a place in The 147th Open as well as the 2018 Masters, Haotong Li was surprised and delighted in equal measure. "That big gift. Huge. Huge," said the 21-year-old Chinese player in his broken English.

Midway through the afternoon, with Li sitting on the clubhouse lead on six-under-par, an even bigger gift had been within touching distance. With Jordan Spieth faltering and Matt Kuchar not pulling away from the field, Li suddenly dared to dream that the Claret Jug could be his for the taking on his debut appearance.

was nonetheless pleased to have put his country on the golfing map in such style. The only previous time that a player from Asia had done better at The Open was in 1971, when Taiwan's Liang Huan Lu finished runner-up to Lee Trevino, also, incidentally, at Birkdale. For Mr Lu read Mr Li.

Li played well from the off. He had rounds of 69, 73, 69 and 63 for a total of 274 that guaranteed him a place at The 147th Open at Carnoustie. His final round was made up of seven birdies, four on the trot from the 15th, and 11 pars.

"It's kind of a dream come true," Li said. "I first started watching The Open when Tiger was around. I always wanted to play The Open and to play so had separated themselves from the rest of the field, finishing six and three strokes ahead of Li respectively after matching closing scores of 69. But this was not quite a duel in the manner of a year earlier when Henrik Stenson and Phil Mickelson had excelled from first tee to 18th green.

"We are going to skip the first 12 holes, right?" Spieth remarked drolly as he entered his press conference. But they provide the context for what was to follow. Spieth, who had not dropped a shot on two of the previous three days, bogeyed three of the first four holes. At the first his drive caught a juicy bit of rough when, for most of the week, if off the fairway, he had an unerring instinct for finding playable lies.

Worse, his putting touch disappeared, a sure sign of nerves taking hold. He three-putted at the third and fourth holes, as well as the ninth. His only birdie came at the fifth, while Kuchar had picked up a shot at the second with an approach to less than a foot. Kuchar dropped a couple of shots but then birdied the ninth and a two-shot swing there meant the pair were level at the turn.

"I just wasn't executing," Spieth admitted. "I was questioning why I could not perform the shots I could before." At the back of his mind was the last time he led a major, at the 2016 Masters, when he was five ahead with nine to play but hit two balls into Rae's Creek and failed to defend the title he had won so brilliantly the year before.

"As you can imagine, those thoughts creep in," he said. "I put a lot of pressure on myself unfortunately, not on purpose, just thinking this is the best opportunity that I've had since the 2016 Masters. And if it weren't to go my way today, then all I'm going to be questioned about and thought about and murmured about is in comparison to that, and that adds a lot of pressure to me."

Ernie Els understands what can happen when you are expected from a young age to win major after major but start faltering. "In 1995 I had a

Ernie Els congratulates Haotong Li on his 63.

Matthew Southgate celebrates finishing in sixth place.

Brooks Koepka putts from off the green at the sixth — the American finished in a share of sixth place.

Alex Noren at the 13th during his final round of 67.

three-stroke lead at the PGA and couldn't get it done. In 1996 I missed out on another very narrow loss at The Open. I kind of stalled. I only got four. But if you get momentum going the other way, then you can go and win a boatload."

With the leaders on the back nine, McIlroy saw what was unfolding and was generously supportive of Spieth. "Going out with a three-shot lead in a major really isn't that much," he said, "especially on a course like this where things can happen so quickly. But he's a fighter, he's shown that his whole career. He can dig himself out and it will be fun to watch. It would be great for the game if he could do it. He's an absolute star and it would be great to see him win another."

Golf tournaments are littered with leaders dropping inexorably down the leaderboard on the final day. One thing that separates the greatest players from the rest is their ability to arrest such a decline

A day after his record 62, the putts did not drop for Branden Grace, as here at the third green.

mid-round. To do so when it matters most is even more rare. What Spieth did next could perhaps only be matched by Nick Faldo at Muirfield in 1992.

Then, the English knight-to-be was four ahead at the start of the final round but found himself two behind after bogeys at the 13th and 14th holes. "You have to play the best four holes of your life," he said to himself — and did. But he was left an emotional wreck. "It's the enormity of it all," he gasped. "The pressure was so great. To end up losing, it would have needed a very big plaster to patch it up. It went from almost a disaster to the absolute ultimate."

"I was so confident," Spieth said now, "and all of a sudden the wheels have come off everything. How do we get back on track and salvage this round, just give yourself a chance at the end. It took a bogey to do so."

Not just any bogey — as he admitted himself, a

A fine defence of his title but 11th place for Henrik Stenson.

It took only four holes for Matt Kuchar to draw level with Spieth for the first time.

Ross Fisher finds himself out of position at the first.

routine five at the 13th would have only made the situation worse — but one of the most extraordinary ever compiled. His drive was so bad that Spieth instantly put his hands to his head and then outstretched an arm to the right as the ball sailed more than 60 yards off line.

There it hit on the head a spectator who was standing on top of one of Birkdale's massive sand dunes, deflecting the ball farther away from the fairway on the other side of the dune. Though the ball was found quickly, and Spieth instantly assessed he would need to take an unplayable because he had no chance to get back to the fairway from his lie, the drop took a while to sort out.

In fact, it took almost 20 minutes, but the most remarkable thing about it was that Spieth was the calmest person amidst the mayhem as he coordinated with the walking referee, David Bonsall, and a roving referee, John Paramor, marshalling

Spieth reacts to his drive at the 13th hole sailing into the dunes on the right.

Spieth asks referee David Bonsall about dropping on the practice range.

"The leaderboard tells us Spieth won the Claret Jug by the same three-shot margin with which he began the final day, but goodness, this was as far from the procession predicted as can possibly be imagined."

—Derek Lawrenson,
Daily Mail

"The storyline was like a warped novel, playing with our minds. Not like golf at all, not sedate; certainly not straightforward."

—Philip Reid,
The Irish Times

"On the verge of another melt-down in a major, so wild off the tee that he played one shot from the driving range at Royal Birkdale and lost the lead for the first time all weekend, Spieth bounced back with a collection of clutch shots, delivering a rally that ranks among the best."

—Doug Ferguson,
Associated Press

"It took him 29 exhausting minutes to make the bogey heard 'round the world.'"

—Michael Bamberger,
Sports Illustrated

Referee John Paramor assists Spieth with his line-of-sight drop on the practice range.

Caddie Michael Greller and Spieth work out an approximate yardage for his third shot.

Hitting blind over the dunes, Spieth finally plays his approach at the 13th before securing a bogey (below).

the crowd and running up and down the dune more than once.

The plan was to go back in line with the hole, which enabled him to reach the practice range, an integral part of the course. He first took unplayable-ball relief, under penalty of one stroke, in amongst the huge equipment manufacturers' trucks and then he took a free drop for line-of-sight relief from the vehicles. "I've hit into a lot of places before," Spieth joked when asked about his presence of mind to find the best escape route.

"I've been in unplayable situations before and just asked the question, 'Is the driving range out of bounds?' And I got the answer, no. I thought that was a much better location for me to hit my next shot because I could get closer to the green and it saved me almost a full stroke on going back to the tee.

"The amount of time it took was trying to figure out exactly where the drop would be, if my nearest point of relief from the equipment trailers would be on the right side of the driving range instead of on the left, where I wouldn't be able to get a lot of club on the ball."

Korean-born American Chan Kim escapes from a bunker at the 17th on the way to finishing 11th.

Li shot up the leaderboard to finish third.

Elsewhere, life was going on as best as possible. On the fairway, Kuchar, not wanting to get cold before hitting his approach, gave himself a birdie chance with a fine shot but then settled down to swap stories with his caddie to pass the time. Up ahead, Richie Ramsay holed out from a bunker at the 17th for an eagle, and McIlroy also claimed a three there to make up for losing a ball at the 15th. The 2014 Champion Golfer finished with his best round of the week, a 67, to tie for fourth place with Scottish Open winner Rafa Cabrera Bello. A stroke behind were Matthew Southgate and Marc Leishman, both with 65s, Alex Noren, Koepka and Grace, whose 70 was eight higher than his record score on Saturday.

Still, it meant a best Open finish for the South African, while Southgate earned the automatic return for next year's Open that he missed out on by a single stroke at Royal Troon. Southgate had returned to Final Qualifying, where he won for the third time in four years, but he will be able to

Austin Connelly plays from sand at the seventh, while Richie Ramsay eagled the 17th from a bunker.

bypass that stage next year. On his defence, Troon winner Stenson tied for 11th with Paul Casey and Chan Kim, while Austin Connelly, the 20-year-old rookie, finished 14th alongside Ian Poulter, Zach Johnson and Hideki Matsuyama, among others.

Back at the 13th, Spieth's problem now was to get a yardage for his next shot. His caddie, Michael Greller, guessed between 230-240 yards and Spieth shelved his three-wood and hit a three-iron instead. It was a strange scene with photographers massed around the player, the trucks just to the side and Spieth hitting over the dunes. Incredibly his shot came up just short of the green and avoided the bunkers.

He still faced a challenging chip over the edge of a bunker, which, after landing on a downslope, trickled on past the hole. Then he holed a putt from eight feet to complete a high tariff up-and-down — somewhat overshadowed by what had gone before — and a miraculous five for the hole.

Kuchar, to whom Spieth apologised profusely

Zach Johnson finished with a second 66 of the week.

Kuchar still had hopes of catching Spieth until he found a greenside bunker at the 18th hole.

Another strong Open finish for Marc Leishman.

for taking so long, just missed his birdie putt so only led by one when it appeared for so long that he might go even further ahead. The time taken was not an issue for the 39-year-old Ryder Cup man. "It was not anything I was ever going to get upset with," he said. "It was understandable, a very difficult situation."

The combination of being behind, but only going one behind, suddenly gave Spieth a lift. "I felt a lot more comfortable having made a putt that I felt really mattered," he said. "It was enough to say this was a new scenario, I had become the challenger and not the leader. My caddie, Michael, said, 'That's a momentum shift right there,' and he was dead on."

Quite how much the dynamics had changed was obvious at the next, the 201-yard par-three 14th hole. Kuchar hit to two-putt territory but Spieth

Spieth holed from 55 feet for an eagle at the 15th hole to reclaim the lead on his own...

almost holed his six-iron and then made his two from four feet. "All of a sudden I felt and believed that I would win, when 30 minutes prior, and really since the fourth hole, I didn't feel that way."

Kuchar got his birdie at the 15th, but Spieth was moving into overdrive. His three-wood to the green finished 55 feet from the hole, but in the putt went. Perhaps Spieth was as stunned as everyone else because he pointed at the hole and then shouted at his caddie: "Go get that!"

"It was an old school move from when caddies used to get the ball out of the hole," he said, explaining that he had been watching the videos of past Championships that run on the televisions around the site. "I didn't really know what I was doing. If I had a redo, I'd give it a big fist pump."

At the 16th, Spieth holed from 25 feet for a birdie and had become an unstoppable force. "Early in the round all those three-footers were 10-footers to me," he said. "And all of a sudden the lid came

...then shouted at his caddie: 'Go get that!'

Round of the Day: *Jordan Spieth – 69*

off, the 30-footers were like two-footers to me. I don't know why I can't make it a little more boring sometimes."

Both players birdied the par-five 17th, Kuchar bravely holing from 15 feet to keep the pressure on but still down by two going to the last. There he found a greenside bunker and ended up with a bogey, while Spieth did his most boring thing for over an hour and two-putted for his par.

Spieth and Kuchar embrace at the 18th.

Gracious as ever, Kuchar did not bemoan the breaks that went the way of his compatriot. "That's part of the game," he said. "We all get our breaks. Nothing I can do about what happens to him, though I certainly muttered under my breath a few times. I feel like you play long enough, these things even out. Sure, he got some breaks, but that's golf."

With the lead in a major with five holes to play, Kuchar played the next four in two under and still lost three shots to his opponent, a cruel blow. "Matt didn't lose the tournament at all today," Spieth said. "He played well down the stretch, I just had my long putts go in, he didn't. I believe he will win a major championship and that he'll do it sometime soon. He's a great champion and a great person."

Even though he won two majors in 2015, only now did the significance of such an achievement sink in for Spieth. "Things happened quickly back then, and until you hit a low, you don't appreciate the highs so much.

"Closing today was extremely important for the way I look at myself, and I'm going to enjoy it more than anything that I've accomplished in the past."

Becoming a Champion Golfer of the Year, especially when fought so hard for as Jordan Spieth did at Royal Birkdale in 2017, is something to enjoy for ever.

Kuchar with the Silver Salver as runner-up.

Alfie Plant with the Silver Medal as the leading amateur.

Teary surprise for gracious Kuchar

While Matt Kuchar beamed with pride at winning an Olympic bronze medal at the Rio Games in 2016, his runner-up finish in The 146th Open, his best finish in a major championship, was bittersweet.

"It's crushing," he said.

"You work so hard to get to this position and it's a thrill to have played well, put up a fight and have a chance to make history and win a Championship. To be this close, to taste it with five holes to go, it's a hard one to take."

Kuchar accepted Jordan Spieth's victory with the good grace we have come to expect from one of the game's gentlemen, and he had the consolation of having his family — wife Sybi and sons Cameron and Carson — meet him as he walked off the 18th green.

"I talked to them last night and thought they were in Colorado on vacation. It was a great surprise, a teary surprise. It was great to have loved ones here to share things with. Golf is a selfish game, and what they go through, it's an amazing support to help me try to be my best. It was very cool to have them here."

The American added: "Man, it was exciting out there. The crowds were just fantastic. It was really fun to be in the arena having a chance to put your name on the Claret Jug. As tough as this is to be so close, I'm sure that it will push me harder to try and finish one place better."

FOURTH ROUND LEADERS

HOLE	1	2	3	4	5	6	7	8	9	10	11	12	13	14	15	16	17	18	TOTAL
PAR	4	4	4	3	4	4	3	4	4	4	4	3	4	3	5	4	5	4	TOTAL
Jordan Spieth	5	4	5	4	3	4	3	4	5	4	4	3	5	2	3	3	4	4	69-268
Matt Kuchar	4	3	5	3	4	5	3	4	3	4	4	3	4	3	4	4	4	5	69-271
Haotong Li	4	4	4	3	4	4	3	3	3	4	4	2	4	3	4	3	4	3	63-274
Rory McIlroy	4	4	4	3	4	4	3	4	3	4	3	3	4	3	6	4	3	4	67-275
Rafa Cabrera Bello	4	4	4	3	4	4	3	3	4	4	5	2	4	3	5	4	4	4	68-275

■ EAGLE OR BETTER   ■ BIRDIES   ■ BOGEYS   ■ DBL BOGEYS/WORSE

This is as much of a high as I've ever experienced in my golfing life.
—Jordan Spieth

Everybody around me is doing their best to put a positive spin on it. I played well. I had four good rounds of golf. I was close.
—Matt Kuchar

It would be a dream to win here, but this course doesn't owe me anything. You don't expect to play well here because of what happened 19 years ago.
—Justin Rose

Who knows where Jordan Spieth is going to end? He could go really big. He can go up to the 14 mark in majors.
—Ernie Els

These things happen. You look at Jack Nicklaus. He went through a stretch where he didn't win a major in three years. I'm not comparing myself to Jack. It's hard to win them.
—Rory McIlroy

To qualify for Troon was special and to play well was a bonus. But this was a more professional performance, a lot less sentimental. I'm absolutely thrilled the way I played today.
—Matthew Southgate

I wish I could have done more for the fans because they carried me around for four days. They were truly remarkable.
—Ian Poulter

It sent shivers down my spine walking up the last.
—Alfie Plant

SCORING SUMMARY

FOURTH ROUND SCORES

Players Under Par	25
Players At Par	19
Players Over Par	33

CHAMPIONSHIP SCORES

Rounds Under Par	115
Rounds At Par	59
Rounds Over Par	292

LOW SCORES

Low First Nine

Aaron Baddeley	31
Daniel Berger	31
Zach Johnson	31
Marc Leishman	31
Alex Noren	31
Webb Simpson	31

Low Second Nine

Haotong Li	31

Low Round

Haotong Li	63

FOURTH ROUND HOLE SUMMARY

HOLE	PAR	YARDS	EAGLES	BIRDIES	PARS	BOGEYS	D.BOGEYS	OTHER	RANK	AVERAGE
1	4	448	0	8	48	14	5	2	1	4.286
2	4	422	0	12	54	9	2	0	11	4.013
3	4	451	0	10	51	16	0	0	6	4.078
4	3	199	0	9	58	10	0	0	11	3.013
5	4	346	0	18	51	7	0	1	16	3.896
6	4	499	0	5	49	22	1	0	2	4.247
7	3	177	0	10	57	9	0	1	10	3.026
8	4	458	0	17	47	13	0	0	14	3.948
9	4	416	0	13	58	5	1	0	15	3.922
OUT	34	3,416	0	102	473	105	9	4		34.429
10	4	402	0	12	55	10	0	0	13	3.974
11	4	436	0	9	57	10	1	0	8	4.039
12	3	183	0	7	49	20	1	0	4	3.195
13	4	499	0	9	48	16	3	1	3	4.208
14	3	200	0	8	58	10	1	0	7	3.052
15	5	542	2	45	24	4	2	0	18	4.468
16	4	438	0	12	51	13	1	0	8	4.039
17	5	567	2	34	33	7	1	0	17	4.623
18	4	473	0	4	61	12	0	0	5	4.104
IN	36	3,740	4	140	436	102	10	1		35.701
TOTAL	70	7,156	4	242	909	207	19	5		70.130

CHAMPIONSHIP HOLE SUMMARY

HOLE	PAR	YARDS	EAGLES	BIRDIES	PARS	BOGEYS	D.BOGEYS	OTHER	RANK	AVERAGE
1	4	448	1	53	303	90	12	7	5	4.174
2	4	422	1	49	334	74	6	2	13	4.088
3	4	451	0	43	330	87	5	1	11	4.122
4	3	199	0	48	329	84	4	1	12	3.101
5	4	346	7	89	326	40	3	1	16	3.884
6	4	499	0	26	245	173	17	5	1	4.427
7	3	177	0	47	310	97	10	2	7	3.163
8	4	458	0	63	293	100	8	2	10	4.127
9	4	416	0	58	322	74	11	1	13	4.088
OUT	**34**	**3,416**	**9**	**476**	**2,792**	**819**	**76**	**22**		**35.174**
10	4	402	0	65	313	75	11	2	15	4.082
11	4	436	0	41	320	88	17	0	5	4.174
12	3	183	0	56	291	105	10	4	4	3.176
13	4	499	0	35	271	132	25	3	2	4.337
14	3	200	0	46	320	89	10	1	9	3.142
15	5	542	10	192	220	37	6	1	18	4.657
16	4	438	0	59	291	98	17	1	7	4.163
17	5	567	16	162	220	54	11	3	17	4.766
18	4	473	1	37	312	108	8	0	3	4.182
IN	**36**	**3,740**	**27**	**693**	**2,558**	**786**	**115**	**15**		**36.678**
TOTAL	**70**	**7,156**	**36**	**1,169**	**5,350**	**1,605**	**191**	**37**		**71.852**

It's a FACT

Jordan Spieth became the fifth Champion Golfer of the Year to score four rounds in the 60s following Greg Norman at Royal St George's in 1993, Nick Price at Turnberry in 1994, Tiger Woods at St Andrews in 2000 and Henrik Stenson at Royal Troon in 2016.

Champion Golfer, champion man

John Hopkins says Jordan Spieth is as exceptional a person as he is a competitor

So Jordan Spieth clambered up and down dunes on his way to his third different major championship. At 23, he was the same age as Jack Nicklaus was when he accomplished the feat. Somehow it isn't sufficient acknowledgement of his golfing skills and his performance at noble Royal Birkdale simply to say that he could become the sixth man to win all four of the game's greatest prizes.

Spieth is an exceptional person, too, a credit to the Jesuits who educated him at a private school, rather like an English public school, in Dallas, Texas. He is as bright as any of his predecessors. When it looked as though he would have to take a penalty drop in an unfriendly place on the 13th in Sunday's round, Spieth realised that the practice ground was in play and used that to his advantage.

Having won the Masters in 2015, the young American underwent an extraordinary crisis when defending his title and blew a five-stroke lead with nine holes to play. Spieth lost that day yet eventually recovered, just as he recovered when he fell behind for the first time all weekend at Birkdale.

He is as good a putter (from six feet or more) as anyone who ever lived, wilder off the tee than many lesser golfers, yet a magician around the greens. On top of all this, he is grounded in a way that few people are. "That's what I like about him," said Tom Watson, a five-time Champion Golfer. "I like his little bit of temper and I like that he is grounded."

What makes Spieth grounded is Ellie, his sister, who has a neurological disorder linked to autism. He talks often of how she inspires him. "Ellie is the best thing that has ever happened to our family," Jordan said. There is some endearing footage of the two of them larking around — Jordan taking Ellie's sunglasses and pretending to run off with them — during one of Spieth's practice rounds before the 2017 US Open. "Every time I come home she says to me: 'Did you win today, Jordan? Did you win?'"

Spieth is like Justin Rose in that he has a gift for saying the right thing at the right time. Consider his first words to Matt Kuchar, who had been standing by the 13th green for nearly 20 minutes while Spieth sorted out where he could drop his ball. "Sorry Matt," he said again and again. Later he would say: "Matt didn't lose the tournament today. I mean, I just had my long putts go in. His didn't."

In the summer of 2015, *Golf Digest*, the world's biggest-selling golf magazine, entitled its July edition "The Jordan Spieth issue." I remember asking him how he felt at this accolade, wondering whether he would say it was journalistic hype, totally justified, or somewhere in between? Might he blush? His answer came in one word: "cool". He was neither boastful nor falsely modest.

David Bonsall (above left) was The R&A referee with Spieth and Kuchar on Sunday at Birkdale and he noticed several striking aspects of Spieth's character.

"The clarity of his mind to start with," Bonsall recalled. "On Sunday, on the sixth, he yanked his drive left but quickly worked out that from there the route was up the right-hand side. He knew exactly where to hit it, did so and got his par. Very sharp.

"When he got to his ball on the 13th there were Coke bottles and hamburger wrappers all around. He didn't touch them. He thought they might be

able to give him a line. Smart. And asking if the practice ground was in play? Smart."

Spieth might not have become the Champion Golfer if it hadn't been for the calming presence alongside him of Michael Greller, his caddie. "Jordan was shouting, 'give me a number, give me a number,' when he was getting ready to hit on the 13th," Bonsall said. "Michael just held up one finger as much as to say: 'Calm down Jordan. I will do this.'"

By then there had been the celebrated talk on the seventh tee when Spieth, three-over-par after the first four holes, was struggling to keep the ship steady. It was similar to the "pull your socks up" remarks made to Rory McIlroy by JP Fitzgerald, his caddie, during Thursday's first round. Greller (right) reminded Spieth of the time he had recently spent on holiday in Mexico with Michael Jordan, the legendary basketball player, and the Olympian, Michael Phelps, among others.

"You're that calibre of person," Greller said to Spieth. "But I need you to believe that right now

because you're in a great position in this tournament."

Time magazine in 2016 named Spieth as one of the "100 most influential people" in the US, noting that "...he exemplifies everything that is good about sports."

Indeed he does. He is an exceptional golfer, an exceptional man.

The 146ᵗʰ Open

Complete Scores

Royal Birkdale Golf Club, Southport, England   **20-23 July 2017**

HOLE	POS	Rd	1	2	3	4	5	6	7	8	9	10	11	12	13	14	15	16	17	18			TOTAL
PAR			4	4	4	3	4	4	3	4	4	4	4	3	4	3	5	4	5	4			
Jordan Spieth	T1	Rd 1	4	3	4	3	4	4	3	3	3	4	4	3	4	2	5	4	4	4	65		
USA	1	Rd 2	3	4	5	3	4	4	3	4	5	4	3	2	4	4	3	5	5	4	69		
$1,845,000	1	Rd 3	4	4	3	3	4	4	2	3	4	4	4	3	4	3	4	4	5	3	65		
	1	Rd 4	5	4	5	4	3	4	3	4	5	4	4	3	5	2	3	3	4	4	69	-12	**268**
Matt Kuchar	T1	Rd 1	4	3	4	2	3	3	3	4	3	4	4	3	4	3	5	4	5	4	65		
USA	2	Rd 2	4	5	3	2	4	4	3	5	4	4	4	3	4	3	4	5	5	5	71		
$1,067,000	2	Rd 3	4	3	3	4	3	4	3	3	4	4	4	3	4	2	4	6	4	4	66		
	2	Rd 4	4	3	5	3	4	5	3	4	3	4	4	3	4	3	4	4	4	5	69	-9	**271**
Haotong Li	T26	Rd 1	4	4	3	3	4	5	4	4	3	4	4	3	4	3	4	4	5	4	69		
China	T24	Rd 2	4	4	4	3	3	5	4	5	4	4	4	4	5	3	5	4	4	4	73		
$684,000	T29	Rd 3	3	4	5	3	4	5	3	4	4	4	3	3	4	3	5	4	5	3	69		
	3	Rd 4	4	4	4	3	4	4	3	3	3	4	4	2	4	3	4	3	4	3	63	-6	**274**
Rory McIlroy	T58	Rd 1	5	4	5	4	5	5	3	4	4	4	3	3	4	3	4	4	4	3	71		
Northern Ireland	T6	Rd 2	3	4	3	3	4	3	3	4	4	4	4	3	5	3	6	4	4	4	68		
$480,000	T11	Rd 3	3	4	4	2	3	4	4	5	3	6	4	3	4	3	4	4	5	4	69		
	T4	Rd 4	4	4	4	3	4	4	3	4	3	4	3	3	4	3	6	4	3	4	67	-5	**275**
Rafa Cabrera Bello	T6	Rd 1	3	4	3	4	4	5	2	3	4	4	4	3	4	3	4	3	5	5	67		
Spain	T10	Rd 2	4	4	4	4	4	5	4	4	4	4	4	3	4	3	4	4	5	5	73		
$480,000	T7	Rd 3	4	5	4	3	4	4	3	3	4	4	4	3	3	3	5	4	4	3	67		
	T4	Rd 4	4	4	4	3	4	4	3	3	4	4	5	2	4	3	5	4	4	4	68	-5	**275**
Matthew Southgate	T79	Rd 1	4	4	4	3	4	4	4	3	4	4	5	3	4	4	4	6	4	4	72		
England	T45	Rd 2	4	4	4	3	4	5	4	4	4	3	6	3	5	2	5	3	5	4	72		
$281,000	T29	Rd 3	4	4	4	3	2	4	3	4	3	4	4	3	4	3	4	4	5	5	67		
	T6	Rd 4	4	3	4	3	3	4	3	5	4	3	4	3	4	2	4	4	4	4	65	-4	**276**
Marc Leishman	T26	Rd 1	5	4	4	3	3	5	2	4	4	4	4	2	4	3	5	5	4	4	69		
Australia	T61	Rd 2	4	4	5	3	4	4	4	4	4	6	4	3	5	4	5	4	5	4	76		
$281,000	T29	Rd 3	3	4	3	3	4	3	4	5	4	4	3	4	2	5	3	3	4	5	66		
	T6	Rd 4	4	3	3	3	4	4	2	4	4	4	4	3	4	3	4	4	4	4	65	-4	**276**
Alex Noren	T12	Rd 1	3	4	4	3	4	5	3	4	4	4	4	3	3	3	5	4	4	4	68		
Sweden	T10	Rd 2	4	5	5	3	4	4	4	4	4	4	4	3	4	3	4	4	5	4	72		
$281,000	T15	Rd 3	4	4	4	3	4	4	3	4	4	4	4	3	4	2	5	4	5	4	69		
	T6	Rd 4	4	4	4	3	3	3	3	4	3	4	5	3	3	3	5	4	5	4	67	-4	**276**

⁽ᵃ⁾Denotes amateur

HOLE	·		1	2	3	4	5	6	7	8	9	10	11	12	13	14	15	16	17	18		
PAR	POS		4	4	4	3	4	4	3	4	4	4	4	3	4	3	5	4	5	4		TOTAL
Branden Grace	T40	Rd 1	5	4	4	4	4	4	3	4	4	4	3	3	4	3	4	4	4	5	70	
South Africa	T45	Rd 2	4	4	4	2	4	5	3	5	4	4	5	4	4	4	5	4	5	4	74	
$281,000	T5	Rd 3	3	4	4	2	3	4	3	3	3	4	4	3	4	2	5	3	4	4	62	
	T6	Rd 4	4	4	4	3	4	5	3	4	4	3	4	3	4	3	5	5	4	4	70	-4 276
Brooks Koepka	T1	Rd 1	4	4	4	3	4	4	3	4	3	4	3	2	3	3	5	5	3	4	65	
USA	T3	Rd 2	4	4	4	3	4	5	3	4	4	4	4	3	5	3	5	4	5	4	72	
$281,000	T3	Rd 3	5	4	3	2	3	4	4	3	4	4	4	3	5	3	4	4	4	5	68	
	T6	Rd 4	5	4	4	3	4	4	4	3	4	4	4	3	5	3	4	5	4	4	71	-4 276
Paul Casey	T4	Rd 1	3	4	4	2	4	4	2	4	4	4	5	3	4	3	5	3	4	4	66	
England	T35	Rd 2	4	5	5	3	4	5	4	4	5	4	4	3	5	3	4	4	6	5	77	
$175,333	T18	Rd 3	4	3	4	3	4	4	3	4	4	4	4	4	3	3	5	3	4	4	67	
	T11	Rd 4	3	4	4	3	4	5	3	4	4	4	4	3	4	3	4	3	4	4	67	-3 277
Chan Kim	T79	Rd 1	5	4	4	3	4	4	3	4	4	4	5	3	3	4	4	6	4	4	72	
USA	T10	Rd 2	4	4	4	2	3	4	3	4	4	4	4	3	5	3	5	3	4	5	68	
$175,333	T7	Rd 3	4	4	4	3	5	3	3	4	4	3	3	3	4	3	6	3	4	4	67	
	T11	Rd 4	4	4	5	3	4	4	3	4	4	4	4	3	4	3	4	4	5	4	70	-3 277
Henrik Stenson	T26	Rd 1	4	4	4	3	3	5	2	4	4	4	4	3	4	4	4	4	5	4	69	
Sweden	T24	Rd 2	4	4	5	3	4	4	4	4	4	4	3	2	5	4	5	4	5	5	73	
$175,333	T7	Rd 3	3	3	4	3	4	5	3	4	4	4	2	2	4	2	4	4	5	4	65	
	T11	Rd 4	4	4	5	3	4	5	3	5	4	4	3	2	4	3	5	4	4	4	70	-3 277
Zach Johnson	T121	Rd 1	5	4	4	4	4	4	3	4	5	5	4	3	4	3	5	5	4	5	75	
USA	T20	Rd 2	4	3	4	3	3	4	3	4	4	4	3	2	4	3	5	5	5	3	66	
$128,917	T40	Rd 3	4	3	5	3	4	4	3	4	4	4	4	3	5	3	4	4	5	5	71	
	T14	Rd 4	4	4	3	3	4	4	3	3	3	4	4	3	3	4	5	4	4	4	66	-2 278
Chris Wood	T58	Rd 1	4	4	4	4	4	5	5	4	4	3	4	3	4	2	5	4	4	4	71	
England	T35	Rd 2	4	5	4	2	4	5	3	4	5	5	4	3	5	3	5	4	5	2	72	
$128,917	T29	Rd 3	5	4	3	3	4	4	3	3	4	3	4	3	4	3	4	6	4	4	68	
	T14	Rd 4	4	4	3	3	3	5	3	4	4	5	4	3	3	3	5	3	4	4	67	-2 278
Jason Dufner	T90	Rd 1	5	4	4	3	4	5	3	5	4	4	3	3	5	3	5	4	4	4	73	
USA	T45	Rd 2	5	4	4	3	4	5	4	4	4	4	4	2	5	3	4	4	4	4	71	
$128,917	T18	Rd 3	4	3	4	3	3	4	3	3	4	4	4	3	4	3	5	4	4	4	66	
	T14	Rd 4	4	5	4	3	4	4	3	4	4	4	4	3	2	4	4	4	4	4	68	-2 278
Ian Poulter	T6	Rd 1	4	3	4	2	4	4	4	4	3	4	4	3	4	3	5	4	4	4	67	
England	T3	Rd 2	4	4	4	3	4	4	3	4	4	4	4	2	4	3	5	5	5	4	70	
$128,917	T11	Rd 3	5	4	4	3	3	4	3	5	3	3	4	4	5	3	4	4	5	4	71	
	T14	Rd 4	4	4	5	3	3	4	3	5	4	4	4	3	4	3	4	5	4	4	70	-2 278
Hideki Matsuyama	T12	Rd 1	3	4	4	4	4	5	2	4	3	4	4	3	4	3	4	4	5	4	68	
Japan	T10	Rd 2	4	4	4	3	4	5	2	3	4	5	5	3	5	2	5	3	7	4	72	
$128,917	T5	Rd 3	4	4	4	4	3	3	2	4	4	4	4	3	4	2	5	4	4	4	66	
	T14	Rd 4	7	4	4	3	4	4	3	3	4	4	5	4	3	4	4	4	4	4	72	-2 278
Austin Connelly	T6	Rd 1	3	4	4	3	4	5	3	4	3	3	4	3	3	3	4	6	4	4	67	
Canada	T6	Rd 2	4	4	4	3	4	4	3	4	4	4	3	3	5	4	5	4	5	5	72	
$128,917	T3	Rd 3	3	2	5	3	4	4	3	5	3	4	4	3	4	3	5	4	4	3	66	
	T14	Rd 4	5	4	4	3	5	4	4	4	5	4	3	2	6	2	4	4	6	4	73	-2 278
Xander Schauffele	T26	Rd 1	4	4	3	2	3	4	4	4	4	5	4	4	5	3	5	3	4	4	69	
USA	T45	Rd 2	4	4	4	3	4	5	4	4	4	4	5	4	5	3	4	4	5	5	75	
$104,500	T52	Rd 3	4	3	5	3	3	5	3	3	4	4	4	4	5	3	4	4	5	4	70	
	T20	Rd 4	5	3	4	3	3	5	3	4	3	3	5	2	4	3	3	4	4	4	65	-1 279

HOLE		1	2	3	4	5	6	7	8	9	10	11	12	13	14	15	16	17	18		TOTAL
PAR	POS	4	4	4	3	4	4	3	4	4	4	3	4	3	5	4	5	4	4		
Charley Hoffman	T6 Rd 1	2	4	4	3	4	5	3	3	3	4	4	3	4	2	4	5	6	4	67	
USA	T10 Rd 2	4	4	4	3	4	5	3	4	4	3	5	4	5	4	4	4	5	4	73	
$104,500	T40 Rd 3	4	4	4	4	3	4	3	6	4	4	4	3	4	3	6	4	5	3	72	
	T20 Rd 4	3	4	4	2	5	4	2	4	4	4	4	4	4	3	4	3	5	4	67	-1 **279**
Adam Scott	T26 Rd 1	4	4	4	3	3	4	3	3	4	4	5	3	5	3	5	4	4	4	69	
Australia	T35 Rd 2	4	4	5	3	4	4	4	4	4	3	5	5	4	3	5	5	4	4	74	
$88,000	T43 Rd 3	4	4	4	3	4	4	3	4	4	4	3	3	4	3	5	5	5	4	70	
	T22 Rd 4	4	4	4	3	4	4	3	4	4	4	3	3	4	2	5	4	4	4	67	E **280**
Jamie Lovemark	T58 Rd 1	4	5	3	2	4	4	3	4	4	4	5	3	4	4	5	4	4	5	71	
USA	T10 Rd 2	3	4	4	3	4	5	3	4	3	4	4	3	4	3	4	4	6	4	69	
$88,000	T18 Rd 3	4	4	4	3	4	4	2	3	4	5	5	3	4	3	4	5	4	5	70	
	T22 Rd 4	4	4	3	3	5	4	3	5	3	3	4	3	4	3	5	4	5	5	70	E **280**
Richard Bland	T6 Rd 1	4	4	4	3	4	5	2	4	4	4	4	3	4	3	5	3	4	3	67	
England	T6 Rd 2	4	3	4	2	4	5	3	5	4	4	4	3	6	2	6	4	5	4	72	
$88,000	T15 Rd 3	5	4	5	3	4	4	3	4	3	4	4	3	4	3	5	4	4	5	70	
	T22 Rd 4	5	4	5	2	4	5	4	3	3	4	4	3	4	3	4	4	6	4	71	E **280**
Rickie Fowler	T58 Rd 1	4	4	4	2	4	5	2	4	3	5	4	4	4	3	6	3	5	5	71	
USA	T24 Rd 2	4	4	4	3	4	3	2	5	4	5	4	4	4	3	5	4	5	4	71	
$88,000	T15 Rd 3	4	4	4	3	2	4	3	4	4	4	4	3	4	3	4	4	4	5	67	
	T22 Rd 4	4	4	4	3	3	4	3	5	3	5	4	3	5	3	4	5	5	4	71	E **280**
Richie Ramsay	T12 Rd 1	4	4	4	3	4	5	2	4	4	4	4	3	5	3	5	3	5	4	68	
Scotland	5 Rd 2	4	4	4	3	4	4	3	4	4	4	3	5	3	5	4	4	4	4	70	
$88,000	T11 Rd 3	5	3	4	2	4	5	3	4	4	5	4	4	3	5	4	4	4	3	70	
	T22 Rd 4	3	5	4	4	4	6	3	4	4	5	4	3	4	3	4	4	3	5	72	E **280**
Aaron Baddeley	T26 Rd 1	3	4	4	2	4	4	3	4	5	4	4	3	5	2	5	4	5	4	69	
Australia	T61 Rd 2	3	4	6	3	3	6	3	4	5	3	4	6	5	3	5	4	5	4	76	
$64,500	T75 Rd 3	5	4	4	3	4	5	3	5	4	3	4	3	4	3	5	4	5	4	72	
	T27 Rd 4	3	3	5	4	4	3	2	4	3	4	4	3	4	3	4	3	4	4	64	+1 **281**
Daniel Berger	T12 Rd 1	4	4	3	4	5	4	2	4	5	3	4	2	4	3	5	4	4	4	68	
USA	T45 Rd 2	4	4	4	3	4	4	4	5	5	5	4	4	4	5	4	4	5	4	76	
$64,500	T52 Rd 3	4	4	4	3	4	5	3	4	4	4	4	3	4	3	5	4	4	4	70	
	T27 Rd 4	4	4	4	3	4	3	2	4	3	5	4	3	5	3	4	4	4	4	67	+1 **281**
Lee Westwood	T58 Rd 1	4	4	4	3	4	4	4	4	4	3	5	2	4	3	6	4	5	4	71	
England	T61 Rd 2	4	5	4	3	2	4	3	5	5	5	5	3	5	3	4	4	6	4	74	
$64,500	T52 Rd 3	4	4	4	3	3	3	3	4	3	4	4	5	4	3	5	4	5	4	69	
	T27 Rd 4	4	3	5	3	4	5	3	3	3	4	4	3	4	4	4	3	5	3	67	+1 **281**
Bubba Watson	T12 Rd 1	4	4	5	3	4	3	3	3	4	4	5	2	5	2	5	4	4	4	68	
USA	T10 Rd 2	4	3	4	3	4	3	4	5	5	6	4	2	4	5	4	3	5	4	72	
$64,500	T29 Rd 3	4	4	4	3	4	4	2	5	4	4	4	3	3	4	6	6	4	4	71	
	T27 Rd 4	4	4	4	3	4	5	4	5	4	3	3	3	3	4	5	5	4	4	70	+1 **281**
Thongchai Jaidee	T40 Rd 1	6	4	4	3	4	4	3	4	3	4	4	3	3	4	4	5	4	4	70	
Thailand	T35 Rd 2	5	4	4	3	4	4	3	4	4	4	5	4	6	3	4	4	4	4	73	
$64,500	T29 Rd 3	4	4	4	3	3	4	3	3	4	4	4	4	3	4	5	4	4	4	68	
	T27 Rd 4	5	4	4	3	3	4	3	4	4	4	4	4	3	3	5	5	4	4	70	+1 **281**
David Drysdale	T79 Rd 1	4	5	4	2	4	5	3	4	4	4	4	3	4	4	5	4	5	4	72	
Scotland	T61 Rd 2	4	4	4	3	4	5	2	5	4	3	4	4	5	2	5	5	6	4	73	
$64,500	T29 Rd 3	5	4	4	3	3	4	2	4	3	4	4	3	3	3	4	4	4	5	66	
	T27 Rd 4	4	4	4	3	4	4	2	5	4	5	3	3	4	3	5	4	5	4	70	+1 **281**

HOLE			1	2	3	4	5	6	7	8	9	10	11	12	13	14	15	16	17	18		
PAR	POS		4	4	4	3	4	4	3	4	4	4	4	3	4	3	5	4	5	4		TOTAL
Tommy Fleetwood	T133	Rd 1	4	4	5	3	4	5	3	4	6	4	4	3	4	3	5	5	6	4	76	
England	T61	Rd 2	4	4	4	3	4	4	3	4	4	4	3	3	5	3	4	4	5	4	69	
$64,500	T29	Rd 3	5	3	4	3	3	4	3	3	5	4	4	3	4	2	3	4	5	4	66	
	T27	Rd 4	4	4	4	3	4	4	3	4	4	4	4	4	4	4	3	5	4	70	+1	**281**
Andrew Johnston	T26	Rd 1	4	4	5	3	5	3	3	4	4	4	5	3	4	3	4	4	3	4	69	
England	T35	Rd 2	4	4	4	3	4	5	4	4	4	4	4	3	4	3	4	5	7	4	74	
$64,500	T18	Rd 3	3	4	4	4	4	4	3	3	4	4	4	3	3	3	4	4	5	4	67	
	T27	Rd 4	5	4	3	3	4	5	3	4	4	4	4	3	5	3	4	4	5	4	71	+1	**281**
Tony Finau	T40	Rd 1	4	4	3	3	4	5	3	5	4	4	4	3	4	3	4	5	4	4	70	
USA	T35	Rd 2	4	5	5	2	4	4	3	4	6	4	4	4	4	3	5	3	5	4	73	
$64,500	T18	Rd 3	3	4	4	5	4	4	2	4	3	5	4	3	4	3	4	4	4	3	67	
	T27	Rd 4	4	4	4	3	4	4	3	4	4	4	3	5	3	5	4	5	4	71	+1	**281**
Jason Day	T26	Rd 1	4	4	3	3	4	5	4	3	4	4	4	2	4	3	5	5	5	3	69	
Australia	T61	Rd 2	4	4	5	3	5	4	3	5	4	4	4	2	4	3	4	6	6	6	76	
$64,500	T18	Rd 3	4	3	4	3	3	4	3	4	3	3	4	3	4	3	4	4	5	4	65	
	T27	Rd 4	6	3	4	3	5	4	3	3	4	4	5	3	4	3	5	4	4	4	71	+1	**281**
Russell Henley	T40	Rd 1	4	4	4	3	4	3	3	4	4	4	4	3	4	3	4	5	5	5	70	
USA	T10	Rd 2	4	4	4	2	4	4	3	5	4	3	6	2	4	3	5	3	6	4	70	
$45,286	T67	Rd 3	4	4	3	3	4	4	3	7	4	4	4	3	6	3	4	4	6	5	75	
	T37	Rd 4	4	4	4	3	3	4	3	3	4	4	4	3	5	3	4	3	5	4	67	+2	**282**
Webb Simpson	T58	Rd 1	5	4	5	3	4	4	4	4	3	4	5	2	4	3	5	5	4	3	71	
USA	T61	Rd 2	3	4	4	3	4	5	5	5	4	4	4	3	5	3	5	4	5	4	74	
$45,286	T67	Rd 3	4	4	4	3	3	4	2	4	4	4	4	3	4	4	4	5	6	4	70	
	T37	Rd 4	4	3	4	2	3	4	3	4	4	4	4	5	3	4	4	5	3	67	+2	**282**
Laurie Canter	T40	Rd 1	4	5	3	3	4	4	3	4	4	4	4	3	5	3	4	5	4	70	
England	T24	Rd 2	3	4	4	3	4	4	4	4	5	3	4	4	5	3	4	4	5	5	72	
$45,286	T52	Rd 3	4	5	4	3	4	5	2	4	5	4	5	2	5	3	5	4	4	4	72	
	T37	Rd 4	3	3	3	4	4	4	3	4	4	4	4	4	3	5	4	4	4	68	+2	**282**
Søren Kjeldsen	T58	Rd 1	5	4	4	3	5	4	3	4	5	4	3	3	4	2	5	5	4	4	71	
Denmark	T24	Rd 2	4	4	4	2	4	4	3	3	4	4	3	5	5	5	5	5	4	5	71	
$45,286	T52	Rd 3	3	4	4	3	5	5	4	4	4	4	4	3	4	3	4	4	5	5	72	
	T37	Rd 4	4	4	5	3	4	4	2	4	3	4	4	2	5	3	4	4	5	4	68	+2	**282**
Martin Kaymer	T79	Rd 1	5	4	4	4	3	6	3	3	4	5	4	3	5	4	4	4	4	3	72	
Germany	T45	Rd 2	4	4	4	3	4	4	3	4	4	3	5	3	4	3	5	5	5	5	72	
$45,286	T52	Rd 3	4	4	3	3	5	5	3	5	4	4	4	3	4	3	5	4	4	70	
	T37	Rd 4	3	4	4	3	4	4	2	5	4	4	3	3	4	3	5	4	5	4	68	+2	**282**
Steve Stricker	T40	Rd 1	4	5	4	3	4	5	3	4	4	3	4	3	3	3	5	5	4	4	70	
USA	T24	Rd 2	4	4	5	3	4	5	3	5	4	4	4	3	4	3	5	4	4	4	72	
$45,286	T29	Rd 3	4	4	4	3	3	5	3	4	3	4	4	4	4	3	4	4	5	4	69	
	T37	Rd 4	4	4	5	3	4	5	3	3	4	3	4	3	4	3	5	4	5	5	71	+2	**282**
Sergio Garcia	T90	Rd 1	5	4	4	3	4	4	3	4	4	4	4	4	3	6	6	4	3	73	
Spain	T24	Rd 2	4	4	4	4	2	4	3	4	4	4	4	3	5	3	4	4	4	5	69	
$45,286	T18	Rd 3	4	4	4	3	3	4	2	4	4	4	4	3	4	3	5	4	5	4	68	
	T37	Rd 4	4	4	3	3	4	4	6	4	4	3	4	4	4	4	4	4	4	5	72	+2	**282**
Sung-Hoon Kang	T12	Rd 1	5	4	4	3	4	5	2	4	4	4	4	3	3	3	5	3	4	4	68	
Korea	T20	Rd 2	4	3	4	3	4	5	3	4	4	4	4	3	5	3	4	5	6	5	73	
$31,070	T75	Rd 3	4	4	4	2	4	4	3	6	6	4	4	4	5	3	5	4	5	5	76	
	T44	Rd 4	4	3	3	2	5	5	3	4	4	3	4	3	3	3	4	4	5	4	66	+3	**283**

	HOLE		1	2	3	4	5	6	7	8	9	10	11	12	13	14	15	16	17	18	
PAR	POS		4	4	4	3	4	4	3	4	4	4	4	3	4	3	5	4	5	4	**TOTAL**
Yikeun Chang	T58	Rd 1	3	4	5	4	4	4	4	4	4	4	4	3	4	3	5	3	6	3	71
Korea	T24	Rd 2	5	4	4	3	4	4	3	4	4	4	4	2	5	3	5	4	5	4	71
$31,070	T43	Rd 3	4	4	4	2	4	5	3	5	4	4	4	4	5	3	4	5	4	3	71
	T44	Rd 4	4	4	4	3	4	3	3	3	5	4	4	4	4	3	4	4	6	4	70 +3 **283**
Jon Rahm	T26	Rd 1	4	4	4	4	4	3	4	4	4	3	5	3	4	2	4	5	4	4	69
Spain	T35	Rd 2	5	5	5	3	3	4	3	4	4	4	5	4	5	4	4	4	4	4	74
$31,070	T43	Rd 3	4	4	4	3	3	4	3	4	4	4	4	3	4	3	5	4	5	5	70
	T44	Rd 4	5	4	4	3	4	5	3	4	4	4	3	4	4	2	4	4	5	4	70 +3 **283**
Andrew Dodt	T26	Rd 1	4	4	4	3	4	4	3	4	5	4	3	4	4	4	5	3	4	3	69
Australia	T45	Rd 2	4	4	4	3	4	4	4	4	5	5	5	4	4	3	5	4	5	4	75
$31,070	T43	Rd 3	5	4	4	3	2	4	2	4	5	5	4	3	4	3	4	5	4	4	69
	T44	Rd 4	5	4	4	3	3	4	2	4	4	4	4	4	3	5	4	4	5	4	70 +3 **283**
Peter Uihlein	T79	Rd 1	4	4	4	4	4	5	3	4	4	4	5	3	4	3	5	4	4	4	72
USA	T45	Rd 2	4	4	4	3	4	4	4	4	4	5	4	2	4	4	5	4	5	4	72
$31,070	T43	Rd 3	3	4	4	3	4	4	3	3	4	4	5	3	4	3	5	4	5	4	69
	T44	Rd 4	4	4	4	3	4	5	3	5	4	4	4	3	4	3	4	4	4	4	70 +3 **283**
Thomas Pieters	T26	Rd 1	5	5	4	3	4	4	3	4	5	4	3	2	4	3	5	4	3	4	69
Belgium	T45	Rd 2	3	3	4	4	4	4	4	4	4	4	5	3	4	4	5	5	6	5	75
$31,070	T40	Rd 3	4	4	4	4	4	4	3	3	3	4	5	2	5	3	4	3	5	4	68
	T44	Rd 4	4	4	4	2	5	4	3	5	4	4	4	3	3	3	4	4	7	4	71 +3 **283**
Kevin Na	T12	Rd 1	4	3	4	2	4	4	2	4	4	4	4	3	6	2	5	5	4	4	68
USA	T35	Rd 2	5	4	4	3	4	5	4	5	4	4	4	3	4	3	5	5	5	4	75
$31,070	T29	Rd 3	4	4	4	2	4	4	3	4	3	4	5	3	4	3	5	4	4	4	68
	T44	Rd 4	4	5	3	3	4	4	3	4	4	4	4	3	4	3	6	4	5	5	72 +3 **283**
Joost Luiten	T12	Rd 1	4	4	4	3	4	4	3	4	4	4	4	3	3	3	4	4	5	4	68
Netherlands	T10	Rd 2	4	4	4	2	4	4	4	4	5	4	5	2	4	3	5	4	6	4	72
$31,070	T18	Rd 3	6	4	3	4	3	3	3	4	4	4	5	3	4	3	4	4	5	4	70
	T44	Rd 4	4	4	4	2	4	5	4	4	4	4	4	4	5	3	6	4	4	4	73 +3 **283**
Matthew Fitzpatrick	T26	Rd 1	4	5	4	3	4	5	3	3	4	3	4	3	4	2	5	5	4	4	69
England	T24	Rd 2	3	4	4	3	4	5	5	5	4	5	4	2	4	3	5	5	4	4	73
$31,070	T18	Rd 3	4	4	5	3	2	5	3	3	4	3	4	3	5	3	4	4	5	4	68
	T44	Rd 4	4	4	5	3	4	5	3	4	5	5	4	3	4	4	4	4	4	4	73 +3 **283**
Ross Fisher	T40	Rd 1	4	4	4	3	4	4	3	4	4	4	4	3	4	4	5	4	4	4	70
England	T24	Rd 2	4	4	5	3	5	4	3	4	4	5	4	3	5	4	3	3	4	5	72
$31,070	T11	Rd 3	3	4	3	4	3	4	3	3	4	4	4	3	4	3	4	3	5	5	66
	T44	Rd 4	5	6	4	3	4	4	3	3	4	4	5	4	5	3	4	4	5	5	75 +3 **283**
Kevin Kisner	T40	Rd 1	4	4	4	3	4	6	4	3	3	3	5	3	3	3	4	4	5	5	70
USA	T20	Rd 2	4	5	5	3	4	4	4	5	5	3	4	3	4	3	4	3	4	4	71
$25,843	T67	Rd 3	5	4	4	4	4	5	3	3	4	4	4	3	4	3	4	4	7	5	74
	T54	Rd 4	4	4	5	3	3	5	3	3	4	4	4	4	4	3	4	4	4	4	69 +4 **284**
JB Holmes	T58	Rd 1	4	4	5	3	4	6	3	4	3	4	5	3	3	3	5	4	5	3	71
USA	T35	Rd 2	4	4	5	3	4	4	3	4	4	4	5	3	5	3	4	4	5	4	72
$25,843	T52	Rd 3	4	3	4	3	3	4	3	4	4	4	4	4	4	2	6	5	7	3	71
	T54	Rd 4	4	4	4	2	4	4	3	3	4	4	4	4	7	3	4	3	5	4	70 +4 **284**
Jimmy Walker	T79	Rd 1	5	4	4	3	4	4	3	5	4	4	4	3	4	3	5	4	5	4	72
USA	T45	Rd 2	4	4	4	3	3	5	3	5	4	5	5	4	4	3	4	3	5	4	72
$25,843	T52	Rd 3	5	3	4	3	3	4	3	5	4	4	4	3	4	3	4	4	6	4	70
	T54	Rd 4	3	4	3	4	4	3	3	4	4	4	4	3	4	3	5	6	5	4	70 +4 **284**

HOLE			1	2	3	4	5	6	7	8	9	10	11	12	13	14	15	16	17	18		
PAR	POS		4	4	4	3	4	4	3	4	4	4	4	3	4	3	5	4	5	4		TOTAL
Toby Tree	T40	Rd 1	4	4	4	3	4	3	3	4	4	4	4	3	4	4	5	5	4	4	70	
England	T61	Rd 2	4	4	4	2	4	5	4	5	4	5	5	3	6	3	5	3	5	4	75	
$25,843	T52	Rd 3	4	4	4	4	4	4	3	4	5	3	3	3	3	3	4	5	5	4	69	
	T54	Rd 4	4	4	4	3	4	4	4	4	4	4	4	3	4	3	4	4	5	4	70	+4 **284**
Justin Rose	T58	Rd 1	3	4	3	3	4	5	3	3	4	5	4	3	4	4	5	5	4	5	71	
England	T61	Rd 2	5	4	5	3	4	5	3	4	4	4	3	4	4	3	4	4	6	5	74	
$25,843	T52	Rd 3	5	4	4	3	4	4	3	3	5	4	4	3	4	3	4	4	4	4	69	
	T54	Rd 4	4	4	4	3	3	4	3	3	4	5	4	3	4	4	4	5	5	4	70	+4 **284**
Scott Hend	T58	Rd 1	4	4	3	3	4	5	3	4	4	6	4	2	5	3	4	4	5	4	71	
Australia	T61	Rd 2	4	3	4	3	4	6	3	4	4	4	3	4	5	3	6	4	6	4	74	
$25,843	T18	Rd 3	5	5	4	3	3	4	3	4	3	4	4	3	3	2	4	3	4	4	65	
	T54	Rd 4	4	4	4	4	3	4	3	4	4	4	4	4	4	5	7	4	4	4	74	+4 **284**
Dustin Johnson	T58	Rd 1	4	3	4	3	4	4	4	4	4	4	4	3	4	4	5	4	5	4	71	
USA	T35	Rd 2	4	4	4	3	5	4	3	4	5	4	4	2	5	3	4	4	5	5	72	
$25,843	T7	Rd 3	3	4	4	2	3	4	2	4	4	3	4	3	4	3	4	4	5	4	64	
	T54	Rd 4	6	5	4	4	3	4	3	5	4	4	5	3	5	3	5	4	5	5	77	+4 **284**
Ernie Els	T12	Rd 1	3	4	4	3	3	4	3	4	5	4	4	3	4	3	4	3	5	5	68	
South Africa	T10	Rd 2	4	5	4	3	4	4	3	4	5	4	4	3	4	4	5	4	5	4	73	
$25,000	T29	Rd 3	4	4	4	3	4	4	3	3	4	4	5	4	3	5	4	4	4	4	70	
	61	Rd 4	5	5	4	3	4	5	3	4	4	4	4	4	5	3	4	4	5	4	74	+5 **285**
Thorbjørn Olesen	T40	Rd 1	4	3	4	3	4	4	3	4	4	4	4	2	4	4	5	4	5	4	70	
Denmark	T24	Rd 2	3	4	4	3	3	6	3	4	4	4	5	4	5	3	4	3	5	5	72	
$24,500	T73	Rd 3	4	4	4	3	4	3	3	7	4	4	4	3	5	3	5	4	5	5	74	
	T62	Rd 4	4	4	4	3	4	5	3	4	4	3	5	3	4	3	6	3	5	3	70	+6 **286**
Sean O'Hair	T79	Rd 1	5	4	3	4	4	5	3	6	4	4	5	3	4	3	5	3	3	4	72	
USA	T61	Rd 2	4	5	5	3	4	4	3	4	4	5	4	3	4	3	4	4	6	4	73	
$24,500	T73	Rd 3	4	4	3	4	4	4	4	6	4	3	3	4	3	5	4	5	4		71	
	T62	Rd 4	4	4	4	3	4	5	3	4	4	3	4	3	4	3	5	4	4	5	70	+6 **286**
Charl Schwartzel	T4	Rd 1	3	4	4	3	4	5	4	3	4	3	4	3	3	3	5	4	4	3	66	
South Africa	T45	Rd 2	4	4	4	2	6	5	3	4	4	5	4	4	6	3	6	5	5	4	78	
$24,500	T67	Rd 3	5	4	4	3	4	4	3	4	4	4	4	3	5	3	4	5	4	4	71	
	T62	Rd 4	6	4	4	2	3	4	3	4	4	3	3	3	5	3	4	5	6	5	71	+6 **286**
Mike Lorenzo-Vera	T121	Rd 1	5	5	4	3	4	5	2	4	4	4	4	3	5	3	5	6	5	4	75	
France	T61	Rd 2	4	4	4	3	4	5	3	4	3	4	3	4	4	3	5	4	4	5	70	
$24,500	T67	Rd 3	3	4	5	3	4	4	3	4	5	4	5	3	4	3	4	4	4	4	70	
	T62	Rd 4	4	5	5	2	4	4	3	4	4	4	4	5	5	2	4	4	4	4	71	+6 **286**
Younghan Song	T58	Rd 1	4	4	4	4	3	5	3	4	5	4	4	3	4	3	5	4	4	4	71	
Korea	T61	Rd 2	5	4	4	3	5	4	4	5	5	4	4	4	4	3	4	3	5	4	74	
$24,500	T52	Rd 3	5	4	4	2	3	3	3	4	4	4	4	4	3	5	4	5	4		69	
	T62	Rd 4	4	3	4	3	4	4	3	4	6	4	5	3	4	3	5	3	5	5	72	+6 **286**
KT Kim	T90	Rd 1	7	4	4	2	4	4	3	4	4	3	4	4	4	3	5	5	5	4	73	
Korea	T45	Rd 2	4	4	4	3	3	5	3	5	5	3	5	3	4	3	4	5	5	4	71	
$24,500	T43	Rd 3	4	4	4	2	4	5	3	4	4	4	4	3	4	3	5	3	5	4	69	
	T62	Rd 4	6	5	4	3	4	4	2	4	4	4	4	3	4	3	4	5	6	4	73	+6 **286**
Alfie Plant[a]	T58	Rd 1	3	4	4	3	4	5	3	4	4	3	4	3	5	5	5	4	4	4	71	
England	T45	Rd 2	5	4	5	4	4	5	4	4	4	4	3	4	3	3	3	4	5	4	73	
	T43	Rd 3	4	3	4	3	4	5	3	4	4	5	3	4	3	4	4	4	4		69	
	T62	Rd 4	4	6	4	3	4	5	3	4	4	4	3	4	3	4	5	5	4		73	+6 **286**

			1	2	3	4	5	6	7	8	9	10	11	12	13	14	15	16	17	18		TOTAL
PAR	POS		4	4	4	3	4	4	3	4	4	4	4	3	4	3	5	4	5	4		
Shaun Norris	T58	Rd 1	4	4	3	4	4	5	4	3	3	4	4	3	3	4	6	4	5	4	71	
South Africa	T61	Rd 2	4	4	4	3	4	4	3	4	4	4	4	4	5	4	4	4	6	5	74	
$24,500	T18	Rd 3	3	4	3	3	3	4	3	4	4	3	4	3	4	3	5	4	4	4	65	
	T62	Rd 4	4	5	5	4	4	4	3	4	4	3	4	3	4	4	7	4	6	4	76	+6 **286**
Joe Dean	T79	Rd 1	4	5	3	3	5	3	3	5	4	4	4	3	3	3	4	6	4	6	72	
England	T45	Rd 2	4	4	4	2	4	5	3	4	4	4	4	4	4	2	5	5	6	4	72	
$23,556	T52	Rd 3	4	4	6	3	4	4	2	4	4	5	4	3	4	3	4	4	4	4	70	
	T70	Rd 4	4	4	5	3	4	5	2	5	4	4	4	3	6	2	5	5	4	4	73	+7 **287**
Andy Sullivan	T40	Rd 1	3	4	4	3	4	5	3	5	4	4	4	2	5	3	5	5	3	4	70	
England	T61	Rd 2	4	4	4	3	4	6	3	5	4	4	4	4	4	4	4	4	5	5	75	
$23,556	T52	Rd 3	4	4	4	3	3	4	3	3	4	5	4	3	5	3	5	5	3	4	69	
	T70	Rd 4	7	5	4	3	3	4	3	3	4	4	4	4	4	3	4	5	4	5	73	+7 **287**
Gary Woodland	T40	Rd 1	4	4	4	4	4	4	3	5	4	4	4	3	4	3	5	3	5	3	70	
USA	T6	Rd 2	4	4	4	3	2	5	4	4	4	3	4	3	5	3	4	4	5	4	69	
$23,556	T43	Rd 3	4	5	4	4	4	4	2	5	4	4	5	2	5	3	5	5	4	5	74	
	T70	Rd 4	4	4	4	4	7	4	3	4	4	5	6	2	3	4	4	4	4	4	74	+7 **287**
Brandon Stone	T90	Rd 1	7	6	4	2	4	4	3	5	4	4	4	3	4	2	5	4	4	4	73	
South Africa	T61	Rd 2	4	4	5	3	3	4	3	4	4	5	5	4	5	3	4	4	4	4	72	
$23,556	T43	Rd 3	3	5	5	3	3	4	3	4	4	5	4	3	4	3	5	3	3	4	68	
	T70	Rd 4	6	3	5	3	4	4	4	4	4	4	5	4	4	3	5	4	4	4	74	+7 **287**
Bernd Wiesberger	T26	Rd 1	4	4	5	3	4	4	3	4	4	5	4	2	4	2	5	4	4	4	69	
Austria	T45	Rd 2	5	4	4	3	4	4	4	5	5	5	4	3	6	4	4	3	4	4	75	
$23,163	T67	Rd 3	4	5	4	4	4	4	3	4	3	4	5	4	2	5	4	4	4	4	71	
	T74	Rd 4	5	4	4	3	4	4	3	4	5	5	4	3	4	4	4	4	5	4	73	+8 **288**
James Hahn	T12	Rd 1	4	5	3	3	4	4	3	3	4	4	3	3	4	2	7	4	5	3	68	
USA	T45	Rd 2	4	5	4	5	4	4	3	4	4	4	4	4	4	4	5	4	5	5	76	
$23,163	T52	Rd 3	4	4	4	3	5	4	3	4	4	4	4	5	4	2	4	4	4	4	70	
	T74	Rd 4	5	4	4	3	5	4	3	4	4	4	4	3	5	3	5	5	5	4	74	+8 **288**
Danny Willett	T58	Rd 1	4	3	4	4	4	5	5	4	4	3	4	3	5	4	4	4	3	4	71	
England	T61	Rd 2	4	5	4	3	4	4	3	4	5	3	5	3	4	3	5	4	8	3	74	
$22,975	77	Rd 3	4	4	4	3	4	5	3	4	5	4	4	3	5	3	5	4	5	4	73	
	76	Rd 4	3	4	4	3	3	4	4	5	4	5	4	4	3	4	4	4	5	4	71	+9 **289**
Kent Bulle	T12	Rd 1	4	4	4	3	4	4	3	4	4	3	4	3	5	3	5	4	4	3	68	
USA	T10	Rd 2	3	4	4	3	4	4	3	4	5	4	5	3	5	3	4	5	5	4	72	
$22,850	T52	Rd 3	4	4	4	3	6	5	4	5	3	4	4	3	4	3	4	5	5	4	74	
	77	Rd 4	5	4	4	4	4	4	3	4	4	4	4	4	6	3	5	4	6	4	76	+10 **290**

(Leading 10 professionals and ties receive $7,200 each, next 20 professionals and ties receive $5,750 each, remainder of professionals receive $4,850 each.)

HOLE			1	2	3	4	5	6	7	8	9	10	11	12	13	14	15	16	17	18		
PAR	POS		4	4	4	3	4	4	3	4	4	4	4	3	4	3	5	4	5	4		TOTAL
David Lipsky	T12	Rd 1	4	3	4	3	3	4	3	4	4	4	4	2	4	4	4	4	5	5	68	
USA	**T78**	Rd 2	4	4	4	3	6	4	3	5	4	4	4	4	6	3	6	4	6	4	78	+6 **146**
Ryan Fox	T106	Rd 1	4	4	4	3	4	5	4	4	4	5	4	3	4	3	5	5	4	5	74	
New Zealand	**T78**	Rd 2	4	4	5	3	4	5	4	4	4	3	4	3	5	3	4	3	6	4	72	+6 **146**
Pablo Larrazábal	T79	Rd 1	4	4	4	4	4	4	3	4	4	3	4	3	4	4	5	5	5	4	72	
Spain	**T78**	Rd 2	4	4	3	4	3	5	3	4	4	5	4	4	4	3	5	4	6	5	74	+6 **146**
Roberto Castro	T133	Rd 1	5	4	5	4	4	4	4	3	4	5	5	3	4	3	5	4	5	5	76	
USA	**T78**	Rd 2	4	4	5	3	5	3	3	5	4	4	4	3	5	3	3	4	5	3	70	+6 **146**
Shiv Kapur	T90	Rd 1	5	3	4	3	4	4	6	3	4	4	4	3	4	3	4	5	5	5	73	
India	**T78**	Rd 2	4	4	4	3	4	5	3	4	4	4	5	4	5	2	6	3	5	4	73	+6 **146**
Alexander Levy	T58	Rd 1	4	4	4	3	4	5	3	4	4	3	3	3	5	3	4	4	5	6	71	
France	**T78**	Rd 2	4	5	4	4	4	5	3	4	4	4	5	2	5	3	4	6	5	4	75	+6 **146**
Anirban Lahiri	T90	Rd 1	4	4	4	3	3	5	3	5	4	4	5	4	5	2	5	4	3	5	73	
India	**T78**	Rd 2	4	4	5	4	4	4	3	4	4	5	4	3	4	3	4	4	5	5	73	+6 **146**
Padraig Harrington	T90	Rd 1	4	4	4	3	4	4	4	4	4	4	6	3	4	3	5	4	5	4	73	
Republic of Ireland	**T78**	Rd 2	4	6	5	3	3	4	3	4	4	5	4	3	4	4	5	4	4	4	73	+6 **146**
Si Woo Kim	T40	Rd 1	4	4	4	3	4	4	3	4	4	4	4	2	4	4	5	3	6	4	70	
Korea	**T78**	Rd 2	5	4	4	6	4	4	3	4	4	4	4	3	5	4	4	4	6	4	76	+6 **146**
Mark Foster	T121	Rd 1	4	4	4	4	4	5	4	4	4	4	4	2	4	3	6	5	6	4	75	
England	**T78**	Rd 2	4	4	4	3	4	5	2	4	4	4	5	4	5	3	3	4	5	4	71	+6 **146**
Julian Suri	T106	Rd 1	5	5	4	3	4	6	3	4	4	5	4	2	4	3	5	5	4	4	74	
USA	**T78**	Rd 2	4	4	4	3	4	4	4	4	4	4	4	3	5	4	4	4	5	4	72	+6 **146**
Adam Bland	T121	Rd 1	5	7	4	3	4	5	3	4	5	4	3	3	5	3	5	3	5	4	75	
Australia	**T89**	Rd 2	4	4	5	3	4	5	3	4	4	4	3	2	6	3	4	4	5	5	72	+7 **147**
Matthew Griffin	T40	Rd 1	4	5	4	3	3	5	3	3	4	4	3	3	4	3	5	4	4	4	70	
Australia	**T89**	Rd 2	4	4	5	3	4	4	3	5	3	5	4	6	5	4	6	4	4	4	77	+7 **147**
Martin Laird	T12	Rd 1	5	3	4	3	4	4	4	3	4	4	4	2	4	3	4	4	4	5	68	
Scotland	**T89**	Rd 2	4	4	5	3	4	5	4	5	6	4	6	3	5	3	5	4	5	4	79	+7 **147**
Francesco Molinari	T90	Rd 1	4	4	5	4	5	4	5	4	3	4	4	4	2	5	4	4	4	4	73	
Italy	**T89**	Rd 2	4	5	4	3	4	4	3	4	4	5	6	3	4	4	5	4	4	4	74	+7 **147**
Paul Waring	T106	Rd 1	4	5	4	3	4	4	3	4	4	4	6	3	5	3	5	4	5	4	74	
England	**T89**	Rd 2	4	4	4	3	4	5	3	5	5	4	4	3	5	4	3	3	5	5	73	+7 **147**
Paul Broadhurst	T121	Rd 1	4	6	4	3	5	5	2	5	4	4	4	3	4	3	6	5	3	5	75	
England	**T89**	Rd 2	4	4	4	3	4	4	4	4	4	5	4	4	3	4	4	5	5	4	72	+7 **147**
Russell Knox	T106	Rd 1	4	4	4	3	5	4	2	4	5	5	5	3	4	3	5	6	5	4	74	
Scotland	**T89**	Rd 2	4	4	5	3	5	4	3	5	3	4	4	4	3	5	4	4	4	5	73	+7 **147**
Fabrizio Zanotti	T142	Rd 1	5	4	4	4	5	4	3	6	5	4	4	3	5	4	4	4	5	4	77	
Paraguay	**T89**	Rd 2	4	5	5	3	4	4	3	4	5	3	4	2	4	3	4	4	5	4	70	+7 **147**
Justin Thomas	T6	Rd 1	4	3	4	3	4	5	2	4	4	4	3	4	4	4	4	4	3	4	67	
USA	**T89**	Rd 2	6	5	4	3	4	9	3	5	4	4	4	2	6	2	5	4	5	5	80	+7 **147**
Robert Streb	T26	Rd 1	4	4	4	3	3	5	3	4	3	4	6	3	3	3	5	4	4	4	69	
USA	**T89**	Rd 2	4	4	4	4	4	5	3	4	4	3	3	3	8	3	6	4	6	6	78	+7 **147**

HOLE			1	2	3	4	5	6	7	8	9	10	11	12	13	14	15	16	17	18		
PAR	**POS**		**4**	**4**	**4**	**3**	**4**	**4**	**3**	**4**	**4**	**4**	**4**	**3**	**4**	**3**	**5**	**4**	**5**	**4**	**TOTAL**	
Brian Harman	T40	Rd 1	4	4	4	2	4	4	3	5	3	4	5	3	5	3	4	4	5	4	70	
USA	**T99**	Rd 2	5	4	5	3	4	6	4	4	4	5	4	3	4	3	4	4	6	6	78	+8 **148**
Kevin Chappell	T90	Rd 1	5	4	4	3	4	5	3	4	5	3	5	3	5	3	4	4	4	5	73	
USA	**T99**	Rd 2	5	4	4	4	3	5	4	5	4	4	4	3	4	3	4	4	7	4	75	+8 **148**
Patrick Reed	T90	Rd 1	4	4	5	3	4	4	3	4	4	5	4	3	4	3	5	5	5	4	73	
USA	**T99**	Rd 2	4	4	4	5	3	5	4	4	4	3	3	5	3	6	5	5	5	4	75	+8 **148**
Kyle Stanley	T40	Rd 1	4	4	4	2	4	4	3	4	5	3	4	3	4	5	5	3	5	4	70	
USA	**T99**	Rd 2	5	4	4	4	4	5	4	4	4	4	5	3	5	3	4	6	5	5	78	+8 **148**
Giwhan Kim	T90	Rd 1	4	6	4	3	5	4	3	5	3	3	4	2	4	4	5	5	4	5	73	
Korea	**T99**	Rd 2	4	4	4	3	4	5	3	4	5	4	4	3	6	3	5	4	5	5	75	+8 **148**
Haydn McCullen	T90	Rd 1	4	4	5	2	4	4	3	3	6	3	5	4	5	3	5	4	5	4	73	
England	**T99**	Rd 2	4	4	4	3	4	5	3	4	4	3	4	4	5	4	5	4	6	5	75	+8 **148**
Jbe' Kruger	T133	Rd 1	4	4	4	3	5	5	3	4	4	5	4	4	4	7	4	4	4	4	76	
South Africa	**T99**	Rd 2	4	4	4	3	4	5	3	5	4	3	5	3	4	3	4	3	6	5	72	+8 **148**
Ryan McCarthy	T133	Rd 1	5	4	5	4	4	5	4	4	4	4	4	3	4	6	4	4	4	4	76	
Australia	**T99**	Rd 2	4	4	4	3	3	5	3	4	4	5	3	3	5	4	6	3	5	4	72	+8 **148**
Ryan Moore	T106	Rd 1	6	3	3	4	4	4	4	4	5	4	4	2	5	3	4	4	6	5	74	
USA	**T99**	Rd 2	4	3	4	3	4	4	4	5	7	4	4	3	4	3	5	4	5	4	74	+8 **148**
Tom Lehman	T79	Rd 1	4	4	4	3	4	5	3	4	4	4	4	2	4	3	5	5	5	5	72	
USA	**T99**	Rd 2	4	4	4	4	4	4	4	4	4	4	6	4	5	3	4	4	5	5	76	+8 **148**
Byeong Hun An	T142	Rd 1	4	4	3	4	5	4	3	5	4	4	4	3	5	4	5	5	5	6	77	
Korea	**T99**	Rd 2	4	4	3	3	4	4	4	4	3	5	2	4	4	4	5	6	4	4	71	+8 **148**
Dylan Frittelli	T90	Rd 1	5	4	4	3	5	5	3	4	4	4	4	2	4	4	4	6	4	4	73	
South Africa	**T99**	Rd 2	3	5	4	4	4	3	3	4	5	4	4	5	3	5	4	7	4	4	75	+8 **148**
Darren Clarke	T121	Rd 1	4	4	4	3	5	5	4	5	4	4	4	3	6	3	5	5	4	3	75	
Northern Ireland	**T99**	Rd 2	3	5	5	3	4	4	3	4	4	3	3	6	3	5	5	5	5	3	73	+8 **148**
Alexander Björk	T121	Rd 1	5	5	4	3	3	5	3	5	4	4	4	3	5	3	5	5	5	4	75	
Sweden	**T99**	Rd 2	3	4	4	4	4	4	3	4	4	3	5	5	5	3	5	4	5	4	73	+8 **148**
Connor Syme[a]	T90	Rd 1	4	4	4	3	5	5	3	4	4	4	6	2	5	3	6	6	4	3	73	
Scotland	**T113**	Rd 2	4	3	4	4	3	5	2	5	5	5	4	7	4	3	5	4	5	4	76	+9 **149**
William McGirt	T142	Rd 1	6	4	4	4	4	6	3	5	4	4	4	3	4	3	5	5	5	4	77	
USA	**T113**	Rd 2	4	4	5	3	3	4	3	5	4	4	4	4	4	3	5	4	5	4	72	+9 **149**
Cameron Smith	T106	Rd 1	4	4	4	3	4	4	4	4	4	4	5	3	4	5	5	4	5	4	74	
Australia	**T113**	Rd 2	4	5	5	3	4	5	3	4	5	4	4	3	5	3	4	5	4	5	75	+9 **149**
Bill Haas	T58	Rd 1	5	5	4	3	4	4	4	4	5	3	3	2	5	3	5	5	4	3	71	
USA	**T113**	Rd 2	4	3	5	4	4	4	3	5	4	5	5	4	5	4	5	4	5	5	78	+9 **149**
Paul Lawrie	T40	Rd 1	4	4	4	3	3	4	3	3	5	6	4	3	4	3	4	4	4	5	70	
Scotland	**T113**	Rd 2	4	5	5	3	4	4	3	5	4	5	4	5	6	3	6	4	5	4	79	+9 **149**
Ashley Hall	T121	Rd 1	3	4	4	3	4	4	3	4	4	7	5	4	4	3	5	5	5	4	75	
Australia	**T113**	Rd 2	3	4	5	3	4	6	4	5	5	4	4	4	4	3	4	4	4	4	74	+9 **149**
Stuart Manley	T12	Rd 1	5	4	4	3	4	3	3	4	4	4	3	4	4	5	4	4	3	3	68	
Wales	**T113**	Rd 2	5	4	5	4	3	5	3	4	6	5	5	5	5	6	3	4	6	4	81	+9 **149**
Emiliano Grillo	T133	Rd 1	5	5	4	3	4	4	3	5	4	4	4	3	5	4	4	4	6	5	76	
Argentina	**T113**	Rd 2	4	4	4	4	4	6	3	5	4	4	4	2	4	3	6	4	3	5	73	+9 **149**
Charles Howell III	T106	Rd 1	5	4	4	3	4	5	2	4	4	5	4	3	4	4	6	4	5	4	74	
USA	**T113**	Rd 2	5	4	6	3	4	5	3	4	4	4	4	4	4	4	4	4	5	4	75	+9 **149**

HOLE			1	2	3	4	5	6	7	8	9	10	11	12	13	14	15	16	17	18	TOTAL
PAR	**POS**		4	4	4	3	4	4	3	4	4	4	4	4	3	4	3	5	4	5	
Pat Perez	T106	Rd 1	5	4	4	3	4	5	3	4	3	4	6	3	4	3	5	5	5	4	74
USA	**T113**	Rd 2	4	4	5	4	4	3	5	5	3	4	4	4	5	4	4	4	5	4	75 +9 **149**
Michael Hendry	T90	Rd 1	5	4	4	3	4	5	4	3	5	4	4	3	4	3	6	3	5	4	73
New Zealand	**T123**	Rd 2	4	5	5	3	4	5	2	5	4	4	4	3	6	4	4	5	5	5	77 +10 **150**
Yuta Ikeda	T58	Rd 1	4	4	5	3	4	4	4	4	4	6	4	3	4	2	4	4	5	3	71
Japan	**T123**	Rd 2	4	5	5	3	4	4	4	5	6	4	5	3	4	4	6	4	5	4	79 +10 **150**
Phil Mickelson	T90	Rd 1	4	4	4	3	4	5	4	4	4	4	5	3	4	3	5	4	5	4	73
USA	**T123**	Rd 2	3	4	7	2	4	4	4	5	4	5	5	4	5	2	4	4	6	5	77 +10 **150**
Stewart Cink	T142	Rd 1	4	4	4	4	5	4	3	5	4	4	5	3	4	3	6	7	4	4	77
USA	**T123**	Rd 2	5	4	4	4	4	5	4	5	4	4	4	3	4	3	4	5	3	4	73 +10 **150**
Jeunghun Wang	T142	Rd 1	6	5	3	3	5	4	4	4	4	4	5	4	5	3	5	4	5	4	77
Korea	**T123**	Rd 2	4	3	5	3	4	4	3	4	4	4	4	4	5	3	4	4	7	4	73 +10 **150**
Prayad Marksaeng	T133	Rd 1	4	4	4	3	4	5	3	4	4	4	4	4	3	6	4	7	5	4	76
Thailand	**T123**	Rd 2	4	4	4	4	4	5	3	4	4	4	4	3	4	3	5	4	5	6	74 +10 **150**
David Horsey	T121	Rd 1	4	5	4	3	4	4	4	3	4	5	3	3	6	2	6	5	5	5	75
England	**T123**	Rd 2	4	4	4	4	4	5	4	6	4	4	4	3	4	4	4	4	5	4	75 +10 **150**
Shane Lowry	T79	Rd 1	3	5	4	3	4	4	3	4	3	5	4	3	5	3	5	6	4	4	72
Republic of Ireland	**T123**	Rd 2	5	4	6	3	4	4	3	4	4	3	4	4	6	5	4	4	6	5	78 +10 **150**
Tyrrell Hatton	T121	Rd 1	4	5	4	3	4	5	3	5	4	4	6	3	4	4	4	4	5	4	75
England	**T131**	Rd 2	5	3	3	3	5	4	4	4	5	5	5	4	4	5	4	5	4	4	76 +11 **151**
Jhonattan Vegas	T121	Rd 1	4	4	4	2	3	5	3	4	5	5	6	3	4	4	4	4	6	5	75
Venezuela	**T131**	Rd 2	4	5	4	3	3	5	4	4	5	6	4	4	4	4	4	3	5	5	76 +11 **151**
Nicholas McCarthy	T106	Rd 1	4	5	3	3	4	5	3	4	5	4	4	4	3	6	4	5	4	4	74
England	**T131**	Rd 2	4	4	4	5	3	5	4	5	4	4	4	4	4	5	4	6	4	4	77 +11 **151**
Mark O'Meara	156	Rd 1	8	5	4	4	4	5	5	4	4	5	5	3	4	3	5	4	4	5	81
USA	**T131**	Rd 2	4	5	4	3	3	4	3	4	4	3	4	4	3	4	4	4	5	5	70 +11 **151**
David Duval	T153	Rd 1	4	5	4	3	4	8	3	4	3	4	4	3	5	3	5	5	6	6	79
USA	**T131**	Rd 2	4	5	4	3	4	5	3	5	4	5	4	2	5	4	4	3	4	4	72 +11 **151**
Luca Cianchetti[a]	T121	Rd 1	4	4	4	4	4	5	3	5	4	7	4	3	3	2	5	4	5	5	75
Italy	**T131**	Rd 2	4	4	4	3	4	5	3	5	4	5	4	5	4	4	5	5	4	4	76 +11 **151**
John Daly	T106	Rd 1	5	4	4	4	4	5	4	5	4	5	5	2	4	3	4	4	4	4	74
USA	**T137**	Rd 2	4	3	4	3	4	6	3	4	5	4	4	6	3	4	4	8	5	4	78 +12 **152**
Callum Shinkwin	T106	Rd 1	4	5	4	4	3	5	3	4	4	6	4	3	3	4	5	4	5	4	74
England	**T137**	Rd 2	4	4	4	3	4	7	2	4	4	6	6	3	4	3	5	3	7	5	78 +12 **152**
Hideto Tanihara	T142	Rd 1	5	5	4	3	5	4	3	4	5	4	4	3	4	6	5	4	5	4	77
Japan	**T137**	Rd 2	4	3	5	3	4	5	4	5	5	3	4	4	3	5	4	5	5	4	75 +12 **152**
Yusaku Miyazato	T40	Rd 1	4	4	4	3	5	5	3	4	4	4	4	3	2	5	4	5	3	4	70
Japan	**T137**	Rd 2	4	4	5	3	4	4	5	6	5	4	4	5	4	5	4	8	4	4	82 +12 **152**
Maverick McNealy[a]	T151	Rd 1	7	4	4	4	4	5	3	5	4	5	4	2	5	2	6	5	6	5	78
USA	**T137**	Rd 2	3	4	4	4	4	5	4	5	5	4	4	3	5	3	5	3	5	4	74 +12 **152**
Darren Fichardt	T58	Rd 1	4	5	5	3	4	4	3	4	4	4	4	3	5	3	5	4	4	3	71
South Africa	**T137**	Rd 2	4	5	4	4	4	5	5	5	6	4	4	3	5	3	7	4	5	4	81 +12 **152**
Billy Horschel	T133	Rd 1	4	4	4	3	4	5	3	4	4	5	4	3	5	5	4	7	4	4	76
USA	**T137**	Rd 2	4	4	5	3	4	5	3	5	5	4	4	5	5	3	5	4	5	3	76 +12 **152**
Wesley Bryan	T106	Rd 1	5	4	4	4	4	4	3	5	4	4	4	3	4	3	5	4	5	5	74
USA	**T137**	Rd 2	5	5	5	2	4	6	3	4	4	3	4	4	6	3	6	4	5	5	78 +12 **152**

HOLE			1	2	3	4	5	6	7	8	9	10	11	12	13	14	15	16	17	18	
PAR	POS		4	4	4	3	4	4	3	4	4	4	4	3	4	3	5	4	5	4	TOTAL
Harry Ellis[a]	T142	Rd 1	4	4	4	4	4	5	3	4	5	5	5	3	5	3	4	4	6	5	77
England	**T137**	Rd 2	4	4	5	4	4	5	4	3	5	4	4	3	4	4	5	4	5	4	75 +12 **152**
Louis Oosthuizen	T151	Rd 1	4	4	4	4	5	4	3	4	4	5	3	3	6	4	8	4	5	4	78
South Africa	**T137**	Rd 2	5	4	4	4	4	4	3	5	4	4	4	3	5	3	4	4	5	5	74 +12 **152**
Matthieu Pavon	T106	Rd 1	4	4	4	4	4	4	3	4	4	4	5	3	4	4	5	4	5	5	74
France	**T137**	Rd 2	4	4	5	3	5	5	3	6	4	5	5	3	5	3	5	4	5	4	78 +12 **152**
Adam Hadwin	T58	Rd 1	4	5	4	3	4	5	3	5	3	4	4	3	4	3	5	4	4	4	71
Canada	**T148**	Rd 2	4	4	4	3	4	5	2	4	5	4	4	6	7	4	7	5	5	5	82 +13 **153**
Sebastian Muñoz	T106	Rd 1	5	4	4	3	3	4	4	4	4	4	4	5	4	4	5	5	4	4	74
Colombia	**T148**	Rd 2	4	4	4	3	4	5	3	4	4	5	6	3	5	4	5	5	6	5	79 +13 **153**
Sandy Lyle	T142	Rd 1	5	5	4	3	4	4	4	4	4	6	4	3	3	5	5	5	5	4	77
Scotland	**T148**	Rd 2	4	5	4	3	4	4	4	4	5	6	5	3	4	3	5	4	5	4	76 +13 **153**
Bryson DeChambeau	T133	Rd 1	7	5	4	4	3	4	4	4	4	4	3	3	4	5	5	5	5	4	76
USA	**T148**	Rd 2	4	4	6	3	4	6	3	4	4	4	5	4	5	4	5	4	4	4	77 +13 **153**
Brendan Steele	T133	Rd 1	5	4	4	3	4	5	4	4	5	4	5	3	4	3	6	5	4	4	76
USA	**T148**	Rd 2	5	4	4	3	3	7	3	4	5	5	4	3	6	3	4	4	6	4	77 +13 **153**
Phacara Khongwatmai	T106	Rd 1	4	4	4	3	3	7	3	5	4	3	5	3	4	4	5	4	4	5	74
Thailand	**T153**	Rd 2	5	7	4	3	4	5	4	4	6	4	4	4	4	4	5	4	5	4	80 +14 **154**
Robert Dinwiddie	142	Rd 1	6	5	5	3	4	5	3	4	4	4	4	3	5	3	5	5	5	4	77
England	**T154**	Rd 2	4	5	5	3	4	5	3	4	4	5	4	4	5	4	5	5	6	4	79 +16 **156**
Adam Hodkinson	155	Rd 1	5	4	4	3	5	6	3	6	4	4	6	4	4	3	5	5	5	4	80
England	**T154**	Rd 2	4	4	5	3	4	4	3	5	4	4	4	4	3	5	6	6	6	4	76 +16 **156**
Todd Hamilton	T153	Rd 1	4	4	4	4	4	5	5	5	3	6	3	4	4	5	5	5	5	4	79
USA	**156**	Rd 2	5	5	4	3	5	4	4	5	5	4	4	4	5	4	4	5	5	4	79 +18 **158**

THE TOP TENS

Driving Distance

1 Chan Kim 322.5
2 Dustin Johnson 322.4
3 Rory McIlroy 321.6
4 Adam Scott 316.1
5 Tony Finau 312.4
6 Kent Bulle 312.0
7 Gary Woodland 311.8
8 Xander Schauffele......310.9
9 Jon Rahm 309.4
10 Ross Fisher 308.3
44 *Jordan Spieth.............. 294.5*

Fairways Hit

Maximum of 56

1 Søren Kjeldsen................37
2 Henrik Stenson.............. 36
2 Andrew Dodt................ 36
4 Daniel Berger.................35
4 Alfie Plant[a] 35
6 Branden Grace 33
6 Paul Casey.......................33
6 Laurie Canter 33
6 Steve Stricker..................33
10 Jason Dufner 32
10 Ian Poulter 32
10 Andy Sullivan 32
10 Brandon Stone 32
59 *Jordan Spieth 24*

Greens in Regulation

Maximum of 72

1 Russell Henley 53
2 Laurie Canter 51
3 *Jordan Spieth 50*
3 Alex Noren 50
3 Henrik Stenson 50
3 Jason Dufner 50
3 Søren Kjeldsen............... 50
8 Chris Wood 49
8 Steve Stricker................. 49
8 Sung-Hoon Kang........... 49

Putts

1 Bubba Watson 104
2 Austin Connelly.............106
2 Dustin Johnson.............106
4 Haotong Li 107
4 Rory McIlroy 107
6 Brooks Koepka 108
6 Jimmy Walker...............108
8 Richie Ramsay 110
9 Matt Kuchar 111
9 Hideki Matsuyama.........111
11 *Jordan Spieth 112*

Statistical Rankings

	Driving Distance	Rank	Fairways Hit	Rank	Greens In Regulation	Rank	Putts	Rank
Aaron Baddeley	293.4	49	25	51	46	29	116	26
Daniel Berger	294.0	46	35	4	47	19	118	38
Richard Bland	284.3	61	28	27	45	34	114	17
Kent Bulle	312.0	6	24	59	41	63	123	71
Rafa Cabrera Bello	296.0	40	30	17	48	11	115	20
Laurie Canter	306.3	12	33	6	51	2	126	76
Paul Casey	302.9	17	33	6	47	19	116	26
Yikeun Chang	269.3	76	24	59	43	47	115	20
Austin Connelly	279.8	73	25	51	40	69	106	2
Jason Day	297.3	36	20	74	44	41	116	26
Joe Dean	304.8	13	21	70	37	74	114	17
Andrew Dodt	300.1	29	36	2	43	47	119	46
David Drysdale	279.9	72	30	17	43	47	117	34
Jason Dufner	293.3	50	32	10	50	3	122	67
Ernie Els	280.6	70	22	68	41	63	118	38
Tony Finau	312.4	5	26	41	44	41	117	34
Ross Fisher	308.3	10	31	14	44	41	121	59
Matthew Fitzpatrick	283.0	66	30	17	45	34	119	46
Tommy Fleetwood	284.0	62	30	17	47	19	119	46
Rickie Fowler	302.3	24	26	41	42	58	117	34
Sergio Garcia	302.9	17	15	77	47	19	120	53
Branden Grace	293.8	47	33	6	48	11	116	26
James Hahn	286.0	58	14	41	63	114	17	8
Scott Hend	303.3	16	23	64	46	29	121	59
Russell Henley	287.4	56	29	25	53	1	120	53
Charley Hoffman	304.4	15	26	41	44	41	113	13
JB Holmes	299.0	32	27	35	42	58	115	20
Thongchai Jaidee	296.6	38	28	27	48	11	121	59
Dustin Johnson	322.4	2	26	41	33	77	106	2
Zach Johnson	278.8	74	25	51	47	19	113	13
Andrew Johnston	299.5	31	20	74	45	34	118	38
Sung-Hoon Kang	293.0	51	31	14	49	8	121	59
Martin Kaymer	299.8	30	26	41	40	69	113	13
Chan Kim	322.5	1	26	41	48	11	118	38
KT Kim	282.3	69	30	17	46	29	119	46
Kevin Kisner	300.4	28	27	35	47	19	120	53
Søren Kjeldsen	266.0	77	37	1	50	3	124	72
Brooks Koepka	302.6	22	27	35	40	69	108	6
Matt Kuchar	291.1	55	26	41	46	29	111	9

	Driving Distance	Rank	Fairways Hit	Rank	Greens In Regulation	Rank	Putts	Rank
Marc Leishman	298.4	33	25	51	47	19	117	34
Haotong Li	300.8	27	21	70	43	47	107	4
Mike Lorenzo-Vera	283.9	64	21	70	41	63	116	26
Jamie Lovemark	296.5	39	26	41	47	19	121	59
Joost Luiten	287.3	57	30	17	42	58	116	26
Hideki Matsuyama	300.9	26	27	35	45	34	111	9
Rory McIlroy	321.6	3	26	41	42	58	107	4
Kevin Na	282.6	67	25	51	47	19	121	59
Alex Noren	298.4	33	30	17	50	3	120	53
Shaun Norris	294.1	45	22	68	43	47	119	46
Sean O'Hair	302.9	17	25	51	43	47	120	53
Thorbjørn Olesen	297.3	36	23	64	45	34	118	38
Thomas Pieters	304.6	14	27	35	46	29	119	46
Alfie Plant[a]	282.5	68	35	4	48	11	126	76
Ian Poulter	285.6	59	32	10	40	69	113	13
Jon Rahm	309.4	9	28	27	43	47	118	38
Richie Ramsay	291.9	52	28	27	41	63	110	8
Justin Rose	295.8	41	25	51	43	47	121	59
Xander Schauffele	310.9	8	24	59	45	34	115	20
Charl Schwartzel	294.6	43	23	64	45	34	119	46
Adam Scott	316.1	4	28	27	48	11	121	59
Webb Simpson	280.6	70	28	27	44	41	116	26
Younghan Song	274.9	75	29	25	43	47	118	38
Matthew Southgate	293.8	47	30	17	47	19	115	20
Jordan Spieth	294.5	44	24	59	50	3	112	11
Henrik Stenson	302.9	17	36	2	50	3	116	26
Brandon Stone	302.4	23	32	10	48	11	124	72
Steve Stricker	283.9	64	33	6	49	8	124	72
Andy Sullivan	302.8	21	32	10	43	47	122	67
Toby Tree	291.6	53	20	74	40	69	115	20
Peter Uihlein	301.3	25	24	59	48	11	125	75
Jimmy Walker	297.6	35	28	27	36	76	108	6
Bubba Watson	308.0	11	23	64	37	74	104	1
Lee Westwood	284.0	62	28	27	44	41	112	11
Bernd Wiesberger	295.5	42	27	35	41	63	120	53
Danny Willett	291.4	54	25	51	43	47	122	67
Chris Wood	285.6	59	26	41	49	8	118	38
Gary Woodland	311.8	7	21	70	42	58	122	67

	Driving Distance	Rank	Fairways Hit	Rank	Greens In Regulation	Rank	Putts	Rank
Byeong Hun An	300.3	13	9	138	17	112	60	95
Alexander Björk	274.3	124	15	26	18	90	58	54
Adam Bland	279.8	94	11	109	18	90	59	69
Paul Broadhurst	282.5	83	18	5	14	141	57	33
Wesley Bryan	256.8	154	14	38	14	141	57	33
Roberto Castro	276.8	112	13	63	18	90	60	95
Kevin Chappell	290.8	43	15	26	20	54	64	142
Luca Cianchetti[a]	293.5	32	8	145	18	90	62	120
Stewart Cink	291.0	40	12	90	21	36	64	142
Darren Clarke	280.0	92	16	18	23	8	66	155
John Daly	275.8	114	11	109	17	112	62	120
Bryson DeChambeau	290.8	43	9	138	19	72	63	133
Robert Dinwiddie	264.3	147	12	90	10	154	56	26
David Duval	280.8	88	6	154	10	154	52	3
Harry Ellis[a]	298.0	21	6	154	17	112	64	142
Darren Fichardt	278.5	103	11	109	21	36	64	142
Mark Foster	251.8	155	20	1	22	20	64	142
Ryan Fox	318.8	2	8	145	17	112	59	69
Dylan Frittelli	283.3	78	14	38	21	36	63	133
Matthew Griffin	279.5	95	18	5	20	54	61	110
Emiliano Grillo	290.8	43	8	145	20	54	62	120
Bill Haas	277.0	111	12	90	20	54	59	69
Adam Hadwin	278.5	103	11	109	18	90	60	95
Ashley Hall	293.3	33	12	90	20	54	62	120
Todd Hamilton	267.8	141	15	26	16	127	64	142
Brian Harman	265.5	144	13	63	20	54	63	133
Padraig Harrington	282.3	85	15	26	18	90	59	69
Tyrrell Hatton	295.8	28	11	109	17	112	65	153
Michael Hendry	275.0	120	8	145	16	127	58	54
Adam Hodkinson	280.3	91	7	152	14	141	61	110
Billy Horschel	291.5	38	13	63	16	127	58	54
David Horsey	277.3	109	9	138	12	152	54	10
Charles Howell III	275.3	119	18	5	18	90	61	110
Yuta Ikeda	290.5	47	17	11	21	36	64	142
Shiv Kapur	260.0	150	13	63	18	90	55	18
Phachara Khongwatmai	287.3	55	13	63	13	150	59	69
Giwhan Kim	265.3	145	14	38	19	72	60	95
Si Woo Kim	275.8	114	14	38	19	72	57	33
Russell Knox	291.0	40	14	38	18	90	59	69
Jbe' Kruger	282.5	83	12	90	18	90	59	69
Anirban Lahiri	296.8	25	14	38	21	36	63	133
Martin Laird	279.0	97	15	26	19	72	62	120
Pablo Larrazábal	283.0	79	17	11	16	127	55	18
Paul Lawrie	283.0	79	13	63	18	90	60	95
Tom Lehman	268.0	140	19	3	21	36	64	142
Alexander Levy	300.0	14	12	90	17	112	58	54
David Lipsky	285.3	69	10	128	21	36	58	54
Shane Lowry	279.5	95	10	128	20	54	61	110
Sandy Lyle	271.5	131	11	109	18	90	64	142
Stuart Manley	276.5	113	14	38	17	112	57	33
Prayad Marksaeng	277.5	107	20	1	17	112	59	69
Nicholas McCarthy	269.8	136	14	38	18	90	63	133
Ryan McCarthy	280.5	89	13	63	17	112	60	95
Haydn McCullen	290.0	49	12	90	16	127	57	33
William McGirt	271.8	130	13	63	18	90	61	110
Maverick McNealy[a]	297.3	22	10	128	14	141	59	69
Phil Mickelson	270.5	134	11	109	14	141	57	33
Yusaku Miyazato	279.0	97	17	11	20	54	64	142
Francesco Molinari	277.5	107	14	38	21	36	65	153
Ryan Moore	275.5	116	10	128	16	127	57	33
Sebastian Muñoz	280.5	89	11	109	15	137	59	69
Mark O'Meara	260.0	150	13	63	10	154	52	3
Louis Oosthuizen	286.5	60	16	18	14	141	57	33
Matthieu Pavon	286.3	62	11	109	13	150	59	69
Pat Perez	265.0	146	9	138	17	112	57	33
Patrick Reed	285.3	69	8	145	18	90	62	120
Callum Shinkwin	300.5	12	12	90	18	90	60	95
Cameron Smith	285.0	72	12	90	16	127	60	95
Kyle Stanley	270.3	135	11	109	22	20	66	155
Brendan Steele	286.3	62	13	63	17	112	63	133
Robert Streb	260.0	150	16	18	20	54	58	54
Julian Suri	278.0	105	13	63	19	72	59	69
Connor Syme[a]	271.0	133	14	38	18	90	59	69
Hideto Tanihara	278.8	99	13	63	18	90	62	120
Justin Thomas	301.3	10	13	63	20	54	57	33
Jhonattan Vegas	289.8	50	13	63	14	141	59	69
Jeunghun Wang	288.0	53	10	128	14	141	56	26
Paul Waring	297.3	22	12	90	22	20	62	120
Fabrizio Zanotti	274.3	124	12	90	14	141	56	26

Roll of Honour

Year	Champion	Score	Margin	Runners-up	Venue
1860	Willie Park Sr	174	2	Tom Morris Sr	Prestwick
1861	Tom Morris Sr	163	4	Willie Park Sr	Prestwick
1862	Tom Morris Sr	163	13	Willie Park Sr	Prestwick
1863	Willie Park Sr	168	2	Tom Morris Sr	Prestwick
1864	Tom Morris Sr	167	2	Andrew Strath	Prestwick
1865	Andrew Strath	162	2	Willie Park Sr	Prestwick
1866	Willie Park Sr	169	2	David Park	Prestwick
1867	Tom Morris Sr	170	2	Willie Park Sr	Prestwick
1868	Tommy Morris Jr	154	3	Tom Morris Sr	Prestwick
1869	Tommy Morris Jr	157	11	Bob Kirk	Prestwick
1870	Tommy Morris Jr	149	12	Bob Kirk, Davie Strath	Prestwick
1871	*No Competition*				
1872	Tommy Morris Jr	166	3	Davie Strath	Prestwick
1873	Tom Kidd	179	1	Jamie Anderson	St Andrews
1874	Mungo Park	159	2	Tommy Morris Jr	Musselburgh
1875	Willie Park Sr	166	2	Bob Martin	Prestwick
1876	Bob Martin	176	—	Davie Strath	St Andrews
	(Martin was awarded the title when Strath refused to play-off)				
1877	Jamie Anderson	160	2	Bob Pringle	Musselburgh
1878	Jamie Anderson	157	2	Bob Kirk	Prestwick
1879	Jamie Anderson	169	3	Jamie Allan, Andrew Kirkaldy	St Andrews
1880	Bob Ferguson	162	5	Peter Paxton	Musselburgh
1881	Bob Ferguson	170	3	Jamie Anderson	Prestwick
1882	Bob Ferguson	171	3	Willie Fernie	St Andrews
1883	Willie Fernie	158	Play-off	Bob Ferguson	Musselburgh
1884	Jack Simpson	160	4	Douglas Rolland, Willie Fernie	Prestwick
1885	Bob Martin	171	1	Archie Simpson	St Andrews
1886	David Brown	157	2	Willie Campbell	Musselburgh
1887	Willie Park Jr	161	1	Bob Martin	Prestwick
1888	Jack Burns	171	1	David Anderson Jr, Ben Sayers	St Andrews
1889	Willie Park Jr	155	Play-off	Andrew Kirkaldy	Musselburgh
1890	John Ball Jr[a]	164	3	Willie Fernie, Archie Simpson	Prestwick
1891	Hugh Kirkaldy	166	2	Willie Fernie, Andrew Kirkaldy	St Andrews
	(From 1892 the competition was extended to 72 holes)				
1892	Harold Hilton[a]	305	3	John Ball Jr[a], Hugh Kirkaldy, Sandy Herd	Muirfield
1893	Willie Auchterlonie	322	2	John Laidlay[a]	Prestwick

Arnold Palmer, 1961

Peter Thomson, 1965

Lee Trevino, 1971

Year	Champion	Score	Margin	Runners-up	Venue
1894	JH Taylor	326	5	Douglas Rolland	St George's
1895	JH Taylor	322	4	Sandy Herd	St Andrews
1896	Harry Vardon	316	Play-off	JH Taylor	Muirfield
1897	Harold Hilton[a]	314	1	James Braid	Royal Liverpool
1898	Harry Vardon	307	1	Willie Park Jr	Prestwick
1899	Harry Vardon	310	5	Jack White	St George's
1900	JH Taylor	309	8	Harry Vardon	St Andrews
1901	James Braid	309	3	Harry Vardon	Muirfield
1902	Sandy Herd	307	1	Harry Vardon, James Braid	Royal Liverpool
1903	Harry Vardon	300	6	Tom Vardon	Prestwick
1904	Jack White	296	1	James Braid, JH Taylor	Royal St George's
1905	James Braid	318	5	JH Taylor, Rowland Jones	St Andrews
1906	James Braid	300	4	JH Taylor	Muirfield
1907	Arnaud Massy	312	2	JH Taylor	Royal Liverpool
1908	James Braid	291	8	Tom Ball	Prestwick
1909	JH Taylor	295	6	James Braid, Tom Ball	Cinque Ports
1910	James Braid	299	4	Sandy Herd	St Andrews
1911	Harry Vardon	303	Play-off	Arnaud Massy	Royal St George's
1912	Ted Ray	295	4	Harry Vardon	Muirfield
1913	JH Taylor	304	8	Ted Ray	Royal Liverpool
1914	Harry Vardon	306	3	JH Taylor	Prestwick

1915-1919 No Championship

Year	Champion	Score	Margin	Runners-up	Venue
1920	George Duncan	303	2	Sandy Herd	Royal Cinque Ports
1921	Jock Hutchison	296	Play-off	Roger Wethered[a]	St Andrews
1922	Walter Hagen	300	1	George Duncan, Jim Barnes	Royal St George's
1923	Arthur Havers	295	1	Walter Hagen	Troon
1924	Walter Hagen	301	1	Ernest Whitcombe	Royal Liverpool
1925	Jim Barnes	300	1	Archie Compston, Ted Ray	Prestwick
1926	Bobby Jones[a]	291	2	Al Watrous	Royal Lytham
1927	Bobby Jones[a]	285	6	Aubrey Boomer, Fred Robson	St Andrews
1928	Walter Hagen	292	2	Gene Sarazen	Royal St George's
1929	Walter Hagen	292	6	Johnny Farrell	Muirfield
1930	Bobby Jones[a]	291	2	Leo Diegel, Macdonald Smith	Royal Liverpool
1931	Tommy Armour	296	1	Jose Jurado	Carnoustie

Year	Champion	Score	Margin	Runners-up	Venue
1932	Gene Sarazen	283	5	Macdonald Smith	Prince's
1933	Denny Shute	292	Play-off	Craig Wood	St Andrews
1934	Henry Cotton	283	5	Sid Brews	Royal St George's
1935	Alf Perry	283	4	Alf Padgham	Muirfield
1936	Alf Padgham	287	1	Jimmy Adams	Royal Liverpool
1937	Henry Cotton	290	2	Reg Whitcombe	Carnoustie
1938	Reg Whitcombe	295	2	Jimmy Adams	Royal St George's
1939	Dick Burton	290	2	Johnny Bulla	St Andrews
1940-1945 No Championship					
1946	Sam Snead	290	4	Bobby Locke, Johnny Bulla	St Andrews
1947	Fred Daly	293	1	Reg Horne, Frank Stranahan[a]	Royal Liverpool
1948	Henry Cotton	284	5	Fred Daly	Muirfield
1949	Bobby Locke	283	Play-off	Harry Bradshaw	Royal St George's
1950	Bobby Locke	279	2	Roberto de Vicenzo	Troon
1951	Max Faulkner	285	2	Antonio Cerda	Royal Portrush
1952	Bobby Locke	287	1	Peter Thomson	Royal Lytham
1953	Ben Hogan	282	4	Frank Stranahan[a], Dai Rees, Peter Thomson, Antonio Cerda	Carnoustie
1954	Peter Thomson	283	1	Syd Scott, Dai Rees, Bobby Locke	Royal Birkdale
1955	Peter Thomson	281	2	John Fallon	St Andrews
1956	Peter Thomson	286	3	Flory Van Donck	Royal Liverpool
1957	Bobby Locke	279	3	Peter Thomson	St Andrews
1958	Peter Thomson	278	Play-off	Dave Thomas	Royal Lytham
1959	Gary Player	284	2	Flory van Donck, Fred Bullock	Muirfield
1960	Kel Nagle	278	1	Arnold Palmer	St Andrews
1961	Arnold Palmer	284	1	Dai Rees	Royal Birkdale
1962	Arnold Palmer	276	6	Kel Nagle	Troon

(Prior to 1963, scores assessed against "level 4s". From 1963, pars were introduced and holes were played in 3, 4 or 5 shots.)

Year	Champion	To Par	Score	Margin	Runners-up	Venue
1963	Bob Charles	-3	277	Play-off	Phil Rodgers	Royal Lytham
1964	Tony Lema	-9	279	5	Jack Nicklaus	St Andrews
1965	Peter Thomson	-7	285	2	Christy O'Connor Sr, Brian Huggett	Royal Birkdale
1966	Jack Nicklaus	-2	282	1	Dave Thomas, Doug Sanders	Muirfield
1967	Roberto de Vicenzo	-10	278	2	Jack Nicklaus	Royal Liverpool
1968	Gary Player	+1	289	2	Jack Nicklaus, Bob Charles	Carnoustie
1969	Tony Jacklin	-4	280	2	Bob Charles	Royal Lytham
1970	Jack Nicklaus	-5	283	Play-off	Doug Sanders	St Andrews
1971	Lee Trevino	-14	278	1	Liang Huan Lu	Royal Birkdale
1972	Lee Trevino	-6	278	1	Jack Nicklaus	Muirfield
1973	Tom Weiskopf	-12	276	3	Neil Coles, Johnny Miller	Troon
1974	Gary Player	-2	282	4	Peter Oosterhuis	Royal Lytham
1975	Tom Watson	-9	279	Play-off	Jack Newton	Carnoustie
1976	Johnny Miller	-9	279	6	Jack Nicklaus, Seve Ballesteros	Royal Birkdale
1977	Tom Watson	-12	268	1	Jack Nicklaus	Turnberry
1978	Jack Nicklaus	-7	281	2	Simon Owen, Ben Crenshaw, Ray Floyd, Tom Kite	St Andrews
1979	Seve Ballesteros	-1	283	3	Jack Nicklaus, Ben Crenshaw	Royal Lytham
1980	Tom Watson	-13	271	4	Lee Trevino	Muirfield
1981	Bill Rogers	-4	276	4	Bernhard Langer	Royal St George's
1982	Tom Watson	-4	284	1	Peter Oosterhuis, Nick Price	Royal Troon
1983	Tom Watson	-9	275	1	Hale Irwin, Andy Bean	Royal Birkdale
1984	Seve Ballesteros	-12	276	2	Bernhard Langer, Tom Watson	St Andrews

Johnny Miller, 1976

Tom Watson, 1983

Ian Baker-Finch, 1991

Year	Champion	To Par	Score	Margin	Runners-up	Venue
1985	Sandy Lyle	+2	282	1	Payne Stewart	Royal St George's
1986	Greg Norman	E	280	5	Gordon J Brand	Turnberry
1987	Nick Faldo	-5	279	1	Rodger Davis, Paul Azinger	Muirfield
1988	Seve Ballesteros	-11	273	2	Nick Price	Royal Lytham
1989	Mark Calcavecchia	-13	275	Play-off	Greg Norman, Wayne Grady	Royal Troon
1990	Nick Faldo	-18	270	5	Mark McNulty, Payne Stewart	St Andrews
1991	Ian Baker-Finch	-8	272	2	Mike Harwood	Royal Birkdale
1992	Nick Faldo	-12	272	1	John Cook	Muirfield
1993	Greg Norman	-13	267	2	Nick Faldo	Royal St George's
1994	Nick Price	-12	268	1	Jesper Parnevik	Turnberry
1995	John Daly	-6	282	Play-off	Costantino Rocca	St Andrews
1996	Tom Lehman	-13	271	2	Mark McCumber, Ernie Els	Royal Lytham
1997	Justin Leonard	-12	272	3	Jesper Parnevik, Darren Clarke	Royal Troon
1998	Mark O'Meara	E	280	Play-off	Brian Watts	Royal Birkdale
1999	Paul Lawrie	+6	290	Play-off	Justin Leonard, Jean Van de Velde	Carnoustie
2000	Tiger Woods	-19	269	8	Ernie Els, Thomas Bjørn	St Andrews
2001	David Duval	-10	274	3	Niclas Fasth	Royal Lytham
2002	Ernie Els	-6	278	Play-off	Thomas Levet, Stuart Appleby, Steve Elkington	Muirfield
2003	Ben Curtis	-1	283	1	Thomas Bjørn, Vijay Singh	Royal St George's
2004	Todd Hamilton	-10	274	Play-off	Ernie Els	Royal Troon
2005	Tiger Woods	-14	274	5	Colin Montgomerie	St Andrews
2006	Tiger Woods	-18	270	2	Chris DiMarco	Royal Liverpool
2007	Padraig Harrington	-7	277	Play-off	Sergio Garcia	Carnoustie
2008	Padraig Harrington	+3	283	4	Ian Poulter	Royal Birkdale
2009	Stewart Cink	-2	278	Play-off	Tom Watson	Turnberry
2010	Louis Oosthuizen	-16	272	7	Lee Westwood	St Andrews
2011	Darren Clarke	-5	275	3	Phil Mickelson, Dustin Johnson	Royal St George's
2012	Ernie Els	-7	273	1	Adam Scott	Royal Lytham
2013	Phil Mickelson	-3	281	3	Henrik Stenson	Muirfield
2014	Rory McIlroy	-17	271	2	Sergio Garcia, Rickie Fowler	Royal Liverpool
2015	Zach Johnson	-15	273	Play-off	Louis Oosthuizen, Marc Leishman	St Andrews
2016	Henrik Stenson	-20	264	3	Phil Mickelson	Royal Troon
2017	Jordan Spieth	-12	268	3	Matt Kuchar	Royal Birkdale

Records

Most Victories

6: Harry Vardon, 1896, 1898, 1899, 1903, 1911, 1914
5: James Braid, 1901, 1905, 1906, 1908, 1910; JH Taylor, 1894, 1895, 1900, 1909, 1913; Peter Thomson, 1954, 1955, 1956, 1958, 1965; Tom Watson, 1975, 1977, 1980, 1982, 1983

Most Runner-Up or Joint Runner-Up Finishes

7: Jack Nicklaus, 1964, 1967, 1968, 1972, 1976, 1977, 1979
6: JH Taylor, 1896, 1904, 1905, 1906, 1907, 1914

Oldest Winners

Tom Morris Sr, 1867, 46 years 102 days
Roberto de Vicenzo, 1967, 44 years 92 days
Harry Vardon, 1914, 44 years 41 days
Tom Morris Sr, 1864, 43 years 92 days
Phil Mickelson, 2013, 43 years 35 days
Darren Clarke, 2011, 42 years 337 days
Ernie Els, 2012, 42 years 279 days

Youngest Winners

Tommy Morris Jr, 1868, 17 years 156 days
Tommy Morris Jr, 1869, 18 years 149 days
Tommy Morris Jr, 1870, 19 years 148 days
Willie Auchterlonie, 1893, 21 years 22 days
Tommy Morris Jr, 1872, 21 years 146 days
Seve Ballesteros, 1979, 22 years 103 days

Known Oldest and Youngest Competitors

74 years, 11 months, 24 days: Tom Morris Sr, 1896
74 years, 4 months, 9 days: Gene Sarazen, 1976
14 years, 4 months, 25 days: Tommy Morris Jr, 1865

Largest Margin of Victory

13 strokes, Tom Morris Sr, 1862
12 strokes, Tommy Morris Jr, 1870
11 strokes, Tommy Morris Jr, 1869
8 strokes, JH Taylor, 1900 and 1913; James Braid, 1908; Tiger Woods, 2000

Lowest Winning Total by a Champion

264, Henrik Stenson, Royal Troon, 2016 – 68, 65, 68, 63
267, Greg Norman, Royal St George's, 1993 – 66, 68, 69, 64

268, Tom Watson, Turnberry, 1977 – 68, 70, 65, 65; Nick Price, Turnberry, 1994 – 69, 66, 67, 66; Jordan Spieth, Royal Birkdale, 2017 – 65, 69, 65, 69

Lowest Total in Relation to Par Since 1963

20 under par: Henrik Stenson, 2016 (264)
19 under par: Tiger Woods, St Andrews, 2000 (269)
18 under par: Nick Faldo, St Andrews, 1990 (270); Tiger Woods, Royal Liverpool, 2006 (270)

Lowest Total by a Runner-Up

267: Phil Mickelson, Royal Troon, 2016 – 63, 69, 70, 65
269: Jack Nicklaus, Turnberry, 1977 – 68, 70, 65, 66; Nick Faldo, Royal St George's, 1993 – 69, 63, 70, 67; Jesper Parnevik, Turnberry, 1994 – 68, 66, 68, 67

Lowest Total by an Amateur

277: Jordan Niebrugge, St Andrews, 2015 – 67, 73, 67, 70

Lowest Individual Round

62: Branden Grace, third round, Royal Birkdale, 2017
63: Mark Hayes, second round, Turnberry, 1977; Isao Aoki, third round, Muirfield, 1980; Greg Norman, second round, Turnberry, 1986; Paul Broadhurst, third round, St Andrews, 1990; Jodie Mudd, fourth round, Royal Birkdale, 1991; Nick Faldo, second round, Royal St George's, 1993; Payne Stewart, fourth round, Royal St George's, 1993; Rory McIlroy, first round, St Andrews, 2010; Phil Mickelson, first round, Royal Troon, 2016; Henrik Stenson, fourth round, Royal Troon, 2016; Haotong Li, fourth round, Royal Birkdale, 2017

Lowest Individual Round by an Amateur

65: Tom Lewis, first round, Royal St George's, 2011

Lowest First Round

63: Rory McIlroy, St Andrews, 2010; Phil Mickelson, Royal Troon, 2016

Lowest Second Round

63: Mark Hayes, Turnberry, 1977; Greg Norman, Turnberry, 1986; Nick Faldo, Royal St George's, 1993

Lowest Third Round

62: Branden Grace, Royal Birkdale, 2017

Lowest Fourth Round

63: Jodie Mudd, Royal Birkdale, 1991; Payne Stewart, Royal St George's, 1993; Henrik Stenson, Royal Troon, 2016; Haotong Li, Royal Birkdale, 2017

Lowest Score over the First 36 Holes

130: Nick Faldo, Muirfield, 1992 – 66, 64; Brandt Snedeker, Royal Lytham & St Annes, 2012 – 66, 64

Lowest Score over the Middle 36 Holes

130: Fuzzy Zoeller, Turnberry, 1994 – 66, 64

Lowest Score over the Final 36 Holes

130: Tom Watson, Turnberry, 1977 – 65, 65; Ian Baker-Finch, Royal Birkdale, 1991 – 64, 66; Anders Forsbrand, Turnberry, 1994 – 66, 64; Marc Leishman, St Andrews, 2015 – 64, 66

Lowest Score over the First 54 Holes

198: Tom Lehman, Royal Lytham & St Annes, 1996 – 67, 67, 64
199: Nick Faldo, St Andrews, 1990 – 67, 65, 67; Nick Faldo, Muirfield, 1992 – 66, 64, 69; Adam Scott, Royal Lytham, 2012 – 64, 67, 68; Jordan Spieth, Royal Birkdale, 2017 – 65, 69, 65

Lowest Score over the Final 54 Holes

196: Henrik Stenson, Royal Troon, 2016 – 65, 68, 63
199: Nick Price, Turnberry, 1994 – 66, 67, 66

Lowest Score for Nine Holes

28: Denis Durnian, first nine, Royal Birkdale, 1983
29: Tom Haliburton, first nine, Royal Lytham & St Annes, 1963; Peter Thomson, first nine, Royal Lytham & St Annes, 1963; Tony Jacklin, first nine, St Andrews, 1970; Bill Longmuir, first nine, Royal Lytham & St Annes, 1979; David J Russell first nine, Royal Lytham & St Annes, 1988; Ian Baker-Finch, first nine, St Andrews, 1990; Paul Broadhurst, first nine, St Andrews, 1990; Ian Baker-Finch, first nine, Royal Birkdale, 1991; Paul McGinley, first nine, Royal Lytham & St Annes, 1996; Ernie Els, first nine, Muirfield, 2002; Sergio Garcia, first nine, Royal Liverpool, 2006; David Lingmerth, first nine, St Andrews, 2015; Matt Kuchar, first nine, Royal Birkdale, 2017; Branden Grace, first nine, Royal Birkdale, 2017

Most Successive Victories

4: Tommy Morris Jr, 1868-72 (No Championship in 1871)
3: Jamie Anderson, 1877-79; Bob Ferguson, 1880-82; Peter Thomson, 1954-56
2: Tom Morris Sr, 1861-62; JH Taylor, 1894-95; Harry Vardon, 1898-99; James Braid, 1905-06; Bobby Jones, 1926-27; Walter Hagen, 1928-29; Bobby Locke, 1949-50; Arnold Palmer, 1961-62; Lee Trevino, 1971-72; Tom Watson, 1982-83; Tiger Woods, 2005-06; Padraig Harrington, 2007-08

Amateurs Who Have Won The Open

3: Bobby Jones, Royal Lytham & St Annes, 1926; St Andrews, 1927; Royal Liverpool, 1930
2: Harold Hilton, Muirfield, 1892; Royal Liverpool, 1897
1: John Ball Jr, Prestwick, 1890

Champions Who Won on Debut

Willie Park Sr, Prestwick, 1860; Tom Kidd, St Andrews, 1873; Mungo Park, Musselburgh, 1874; Jock Hutchison, St Andrews, 1921; Denny Shute, St Andrews, 1933; Ben Hogan, Carnoustie, 1953; Tony Lema, St Andrews, 1964; Tom Watson, Carnoustie, 1975; Ben Curtis, Royal St George's, 2003

Attendance

Year	Total
1960	39,563
1961	21,708
1962	37,098
1963	24,585
1964	35,954
1965	32,927
1966	40,182
1967	29,880
1968	51,819
1969	46,001
1970	81,593
1971	70,076
1972	84,746
1973	78,810
1974	92,796
1975	85,258
1976	92,021
1977	87,615
1978	125,271
1979	134,501
1980	131,610
1981	111,987
1982	133,299
1983	142,892
1984	193,126
1985	141,619
1986	134,261
1987	139,189
1988	191,334
1989	160,639
1990	208,680
1991	189,435
1992	146,427
1993	141,000
1994	128,000
1995	180,000
1996	170,000
1997	176,000
1998	195,100
1999	157,000
2000	239,000
2001	178,000
2002	161,500
2003	183,000
2004	176,000
2005	223,000
2006	230,000
2007	154,000
2008	201,500
2009	123,000
2010	201,000
2011	180,100
2012	181,300
2013	142,036
2014	202,917
2015	237,024
2016	173,134
2017	235,000

Greatest Interval Between First and Last Victory

19 years: JH Taylor, 1894-1913
18 years: Harry Vardon, 1896-1914
15 years: Willie Park Sr, 1860-75; Gary Player, 1959-74
14 years: Henry Cotton, 1934-48

Greatest Interval Between Victories

11 years: Henry Cotton, 1937-48 *(No Championship 1940-45)*
10 years: Ernie Els, 2002-12
9 years: Willie Park Sr, 1866-75; Bob Martin, 1876-85; JH Taylor, 1900-09; Gary Player, 1959-68

Champions Who Have Won in Three Separate Decades

Harry Vardon, 1896, 1898 & 1899/1903/1911 & 1914
JH Taylor, 1894 & 1895/1900 & 1909/1913
Gary Player, 1959/1968/1974

Competitors with the Most Top Five Finishes

16: JH Taylor; Jack Nicklaus

Competitors Who Have Recorded the Most Rounds Under Par From 1963

59: Jack Nicklaus
54: Nick Faldo

Competitors with the Most Finishes Under Par From 1963

15: Ernie Els
14: Jack Nicklaus; Nick Faldo
13: Tom Watson

Champions Who Have Led Outright After Every Round

72 hole Championships
Ted Ray, 1912; Bobby Jones, 1927; Gene Sarazen, 1932; Henry Cotton, 1934; Tom Weiskopf, 1973; Tiger Woods, 2005; Rory McIlroy, 2014
36 hole Championships
Willie Park Sr, 1860 and 1866; Tom Morris Sr, 1862 and 1864; Tommy Morris Jr, 1869 and 1870; Mungo Park, 1874; Jamie Anderson, 1879; Bob Ferguson, 1880, 1881, 1882; Willie Fernie, 1883; Jack Simpson, 1884; Hugh Kirkaldy, 1891

Largest Leads Since 1892

After 18 holes:
5 strokes: Sandy Herd, 1896
4 strokes: Harry Vardon, 1902; Jim Barnes, 1925; Christy O'Connor Jr, 1985
After 36 holes:
9 strokes: Henry Cotton, 1934
6 strokes: Abe Mitchell, 1920
After 54 holes:
10 strokes: Henry Cotton, 1934
7 strokes: Harry Vardon, 1903; Tony Lema, 1964
6 strokes: JH Taylor, 1900; James Braid, 1905; James Braid, 1908; Max Faulkner, 1951; Tom Lehman, 1996; Tiger Woods, 2000; Rory McIlroy, 2014

Champions Who Had Four Rounds, Each Better than the One Before

Jack White, Royal St George's, 1904 – 80, 75, 72, 69
James Braid, Muirfield, 1906 – 77, 76, 74, 73
Ben Hogan, Carnoustie, 1953 – 73, 71, 70, 68
Gary Player, Muirfield, 1959 – 75, 71, 70, 68

Same Number of Strokes in Each of the Four Rounds by a Champion

Denny Shute, St Andrews, 1933 – 73, 73, 73, 73 (excluding the play-off)

Best 18-Hole Recovery by a Champion

George Duncan, Deal, 1920. Duncan was 13 strokes behind the leader, Abe Mitchell, after 36 holes and level with him after 54.

Greatest Variation Between Rounds by a Champion

14 strokes: Henry Cotton, 1934, second round 65, fourth round 79
12 strokes: Henry Cotton, 1934, first round 67, fourth round 79
11 strokes: Jack White, 1904, first round 80, fourth round 69; Greg Norman, 1986, first round 74, second round 63; Greg Norman, 1986, second round 63, third round 74
10 strokes: Seve Ballesteros, 1979, second round 65, third round 75

Greatest Variation Between Two Successive Rounds by a Champion

11 strokes: Greg Norman, 1986, first round 74, second round 63; Greg Norman, 1986, second round 63, third round 74
10 strokes: Seve Ballesteros, 1979, second round 65, third round 75

Greatest Comeback by a Champion

After 18 holes
Harry Vardon, 1896, 11 strokes behind the leader
After 36 holes
George Duncan, 1920, 13 strokes behind the leader
After 54 holes
Paul Lawrie, 1999, 10 strokes behind the leader

Champions Who Had Four Rounds Under 70

Greg Norman, Royal St George's, 1993 – 66, 68, 69, 64; Nick Price, Turnberry, 1994 – 69, 66, 67, 66; Tiger Woods, St Andrews, 2000 – 67, 66, 67, 69; Henrik Stenson, Royal Troon, 2016 – 68, 65, 68, 63; Jordan Spieth, Royal Birkdale, 2017 – 65, 69, 65, 69

Competitors Who Failed to Win The Open Despite Having Four Rounds Under 70

Ernie Els, Royal St George's, 1993 – 68, 69, 69, 68; Jesper Parnevik, Turnberry, 1994 – 68, 66, 68, 67; Ernie Els, Royal Troon, 2004 – 69, 69, 68, 68; Rickie Fowler, Royal Liverpool, 2014 – 69, 69, 68, 67

Lowest Final Round by a Champion

63: Henrik Stenson, Royal Troon, 2016
64: Greg Norman, Royal St George's, 1993
65: Tom Watson, Turnberry, 1977; Seve Ballesteros, Royal Lytham & St Annes, 1988; Justin Leonard, Royal Troon, 1997

Worst Round by a Champion Since 1939

78: Fred Daly, third round, Royal Liverpool, 1947
76: Bobby Locke, second round, Royal St George's, 1949; Paul Lawrie, third round, Carnoustie, 1999

Champion with the Worst Finishing Round Since 1939

75: Sam Snead, St Andrews, 1946

Lowest Opening Round by a Champion

65: Louis Oosthuizen, St Andrews, 2010; Jordan Spieth, Royal Birkdale, 2017

Most Open Championship Appearances

46: Gary Player
42: Sandy Lyle
38: Sandy Herd, Jack Nicklaus, Tom Watson
37: Nick Faldo

Most Final Day Appearances Since 1892

32: Jack Nicklaus
31: Sandy Herd
30: JH Taylor
28: Ted Ray
27: Harry Vardon, James Braid, Nick Faldo
26: Peter Thomson, Gary Player, Tom Watson

Most Appearances by a Champion Before His First Victory

19: Darren Clarke, 2011; Phil Mickelson, 2013
15: Nick Price, 1994
14: Sandy Herd, 1902
13: Ted Ray, 1912; Jack White, 1904; Reg Whitcombe, 1938; Mark O'Meara, 1998
11: George Duncan, 1920; Nick Faldo, 1987; Ernie Els, 2002; Stewart Cink, 2009; Zach Johnson, 2015; Henrik Stenson, 2016

The Open Which Provided the Greatest Number of Rounds Under 70 Since 1946

148 rounds, Turnberry, 1994

The Open with the Fewest Rounds Under 70 Since 1946

2 rounds, St Andrews, 1946; Royal Liverpool, 1947; Carnoustie, 1968

Statistically Most Difficult Hole Since 1982

St Andrews, 1984, Par-4 17th, 4.79

Longest Course in Open History

Carnoustie, 2007, 7,421 yards

Number of Times Each Course Has Hosted The Open

St Andrews, 29; Prestwick, 24; Muirfield, 16; Royal St George's, 14; Royal Liverpool, 12; Royal Lytham & St Annes, 11; Royal Birkdale, 10; Royal Troon, 9; Carnoustie, 7; Musselburgh, 6; Turnberry, 4; Royal Cinque Ports, 2; Royal Portrush, Prince's, 1 each

Prize Money (£)

Year	Total	First Prize	Year	Total	First Prize	Year	Total	First Prize	Year	Total	First Prize
1860	nil	nil	1890	29.50	13	1966	15,000	2,100	1993	1,000,000	100,000
1863	10	nil	1891	28.50	10	1968	20,000	3,000	1994	1,100,000	110,000
1864	15	6	1892	110	35	1969	30,000	4,250	1995	1,250,000	125,000
1865	20	8	1893	100	30	1970	40,000	5,250	1996	1,400,000	200,000
1866	11	6	1900	125	50	1971	45,000	5,500	1997	1,600,000	250,000
1867	16	7	1910	135	50	1972	50,000	5,500	1998	1,800,000	300,000
1868	12	6	1920	225	75	1975	75,000	7,500	1999	2,000,000	350,000
1872	unknown	8	1927	275	75	1977	100,000	10,000	2000	2,750,000	500,000
1873	unknown	11	1930	400	100	1978	125,000	12,500	2001	3,300,000	600,000
1874	20	8	1931	500	100	1979	155,000	15,000	2002	3,800,000	700,000
1876	27	10	1946	1,000	150	1980	200,000	25,000	2003	3,900,000	700,000
1877	20	8	1949	1,500	300	1982	250,000	32,000	2004	4,000,000	720,000
1878	unknown	8	1951	1,700	300	1983	310,000	40,000	2007	4,200,000	750,000
1879	47	10	1953	2,500	500	1984	451,000	55,000	2010	4,800,000	850,000
1880	unknown	8	1954	3,500	750	1985	530,000	65,000	2011	5,000,000	900,000
1881	21	8	1955	3,750	1,000	1986	600,000	70,000	2013	5,250,000	945,000
1882	47.25	12	1958	4,850	1,000	1987	650,000	75,000	2014	5,400,000	975,000
1883	20	8	1959	5,000	1,000	1988	700,000	80,000	2015	6,300,000	1,150,000
1884	23	8	1960	7,000	1,250	1989	750,000	80,000	2016	6,500,000	1,175,000
1885	35.50	10	1961	8,500	1,400	1990	825,000	85,000	2017	$10,250,000	$1,845,000
1886	20	8	1963	8,500	1,500	1991	900,000	90,000			
1889	22	8	1965	10,000	1,750	1992	950,000	95,000			

PHOTOGRAPHY CREDITS

Stan Badz – 55 bottom, 78 middle (2)

David Cannon – 1, 10 second left, right, 16, 18 middle, 22-23, 29, 32 top, 38 bottom, 42 top, 50 bottom, 60 right, 69 top left, 73 bottom, 74 top, 78 third left, 84, 87 bottom, 94 top, 99 top (2)

Chris Condon – 12 second top, 78 top right, 78 bottom right

Tom Dulet – 21 top, bottom left, 78 top left

Stuart Franklin – 10 left, 12 second bottom, 18 top, 20, 32 bottom right, 33 top left, 34, 35 top, 37 bottom, 40 left (2), 42 bottom, 48, 57, 63 right, 74 bottom, 81, 91 bottom, 92 top right, 92 bottom right, 93 top, 97 bottom, 98 top, 101

Richard Heathcote – 7-8, 19, 31, 38 top, 44, 47, 53 right, 58, 67 top, 70, 71, 78 fourth left, 78 second right, 80, 91 top (2), 96 top

Ross Kinnaird – 10 second left, right, 12 bottom, 33 right, 40 right, 46 left, 53 left, 54 left, 89 bottom, 95 top right, 98 bottom, 103 (2)

Matthew Lewis – 4-5, 6, 21 bottom right, 23 bottom, 26, 32 bottom left, 39, 54 top right, 55 top, 77, 82, 92 top left, 92 middle left, 92 bottom right, 93 bottom, 102

Warren Little – 10 second right, 11 left, 13, 25 (2), 28, 30, 49 top, 50 top, 54 bottom right, 60 left, 69 bottom, 75, 78 second left, 90 top, 104-105, 106

Dan Mullan – 12 top, 35 bottom, 36 bottom, 88 top, 95 top left

Christian Petersen – 36 top, 52, 56, 62, 72 top, 78 bottom left, 89 top, 97 top

Andrew Redington – 10 second right, 18 second bottom, 24, 33 bottom left, 43, 59, 63 left, 64, 66, 67 bottom (2), 68 (2), 69 top right, 72 bottom, 73 top, 76, 86, 87 top, 94 bottom, 95 bottom, 96 bottom, 128

Gregory Shamus – 12 middle, 37 top, 46 right, 49 bottom, 78 fourth right, 85, 88 bottom, 90 bottom, 99 bottom

Historical photos on p.121, 123 copyright R&A Championships.

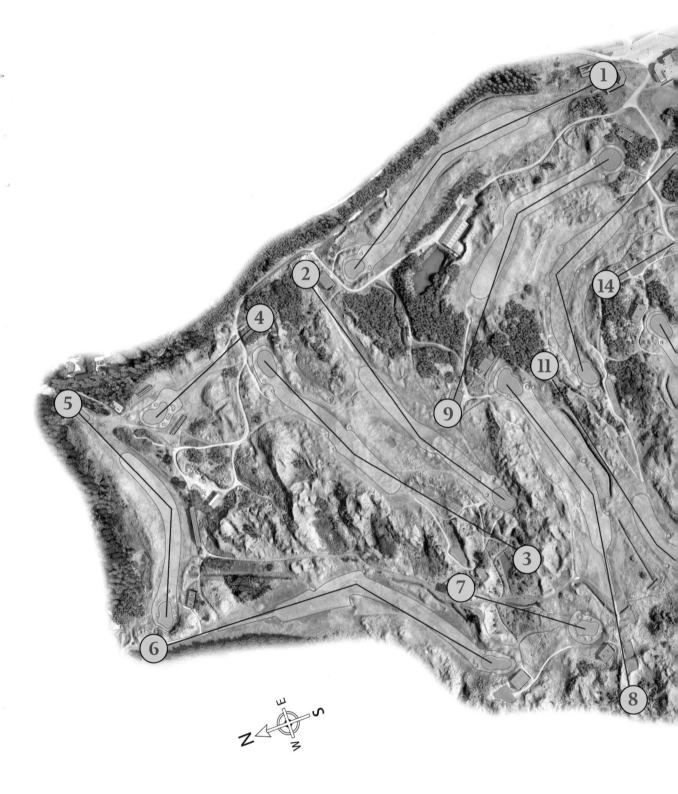